· TROPHIES ·

MOVING AHEAD

Harcourt

Orlando   Boston   Dallas   Chicago   San Diego

Visit *The Learning Site!*
www.harcourtschool.com

CONTENTS

Gram's Plant Parade **6**
by Susan McCloskey

Teacher Read-Aloud **Blooming Riddles** **13**

Click! **14**
by Celeste Albright

A Troublesome Nose **22**
by Linda Lott

Teacher Read-Aloud **The Nose Knows** **29**

Joe DiMaggio, One of Baseball's
Greatest **30**
by Tomás Castillo

Amelia's Flying Lesson **38**
by Celeste Albright

Can-Do Kid **46**
by Kaye Gager

Teacher Read-Aloud **How Silly!** **53**

Small but Brave **54**
by Susan McCloskey

Bringing Back the Puffins **62**
by Caren B. Stelson

Teacher Read-Aloud **Winging It** **69**

Green Tomatoes **70**
by Charlene Norman

A Day with the Orangutans **78**
by Jeannie W. Berger

3

A Home on the Oregon Trail **86**
by Sydnie Meltzer Kleinhenz

Teacher Read-Aloud **Way Out West** **93**

Sisters Forever **94**
by Lee Chang

Oak Grove Picnic **102**
by Carol Storment

Teacher Read-Aloud **Critter Definitions** **109**

A Pen Pal in Vietnam **110**
by Pam Zollman

Wolf Pack: Sounds and Signals **118**
by Kana Riley

Who Invented This? **126**
by Beverly A. Dietz

Teacher Read-Aloud **Just Curious** **133**

The Case of the Strange Sculptor . . **134**
by Lisa Eisenberg

Just Enough Is Plenty **142**
by Sydnie Meltzer Kleinhenz

Teacher Read-Aloud **Barnyard Baloney** **149**

Big Bad Wolf and the Law **150**
by Deborah Eaton

A Clever Plan **158**
by María Santos

Fire in the Forest **166**
by Caren B. Stelson

[Teacher Read-Aloud] **Mix 'Em Up** **173**

A Place of New Beginnings **174**
by Ben Farrell

Desert Animals **182**
by David Delgado

[Teacher Read-Aloud] **Step on No Pets** **189**

School Days **190**
by Susan McCloskey

When I Was Eight **198**
by Roberto Aguas, Jr., as told to Diane Hoyt-Goldsmith

The West Beckons **206**
by Ben Farrell

[Teacher Read-Aloud] **A Song for Gold
Miners** **213**

Purple Mountain Majesty **214**
by Deborah Akers

[Teacher Read-Aloud] **Required Reading for
Western Explorers** **221**

An American Legend **222**
by Sharon Fear

Bug Catchers **230**
by Robert Newell

Air Force Kids **238**
by Sal Ortega

5

Gram's Plant Parade

by Susan McCloskey
illustrated by Melanie Hall

My name is Blake, and this is my gram. Gram adores plants.

Gram plants in any vacant vase. She plants in hats and caps. She plants in cake pans and brass vats. She plants in frames and crates.

Look! One plant is sprouting in a skate with no mate!

"Blake!" says my gram. "Look at the
station on the corner. Do you see what I see?"
"No, Gram. What do you see?" I ask.
"Vacant land to plant!" says Gram.

Gram takes a sack. I take the spade. We go to the station on the corner.

Gram has bulbs in the sack. She takes bulbs from her pockets, too.

"Now hand me my spade, Blake," she says, "and stand back. I have to plant!"

As Gram plants, we attract stares. Recognizing that I am anxious, Gram pats me on the back.

"Blake, aren't you glad we're sprucing up the station?" she says. "I can't stand a drab, bare landscape!"

"Gram, you amaze me! When will the bulbs be sprouting?" I ask.

"In the future," Gram says. "Then we'll see a plant parade!"

At last the future comes to pass!

Gram and I go to gaze at her plant parade. Now it's the plants that attract stares! One man thanks Gram for sprucing up the corner.

"Will you retire from planting now, Gram?" I ask.
"Retire? Not me!" Gram gazes around the square.
"Look!" she says. "I see vacant land!"
Now I want to share Gram's plant craze.
I know a new plant parade is in our future!

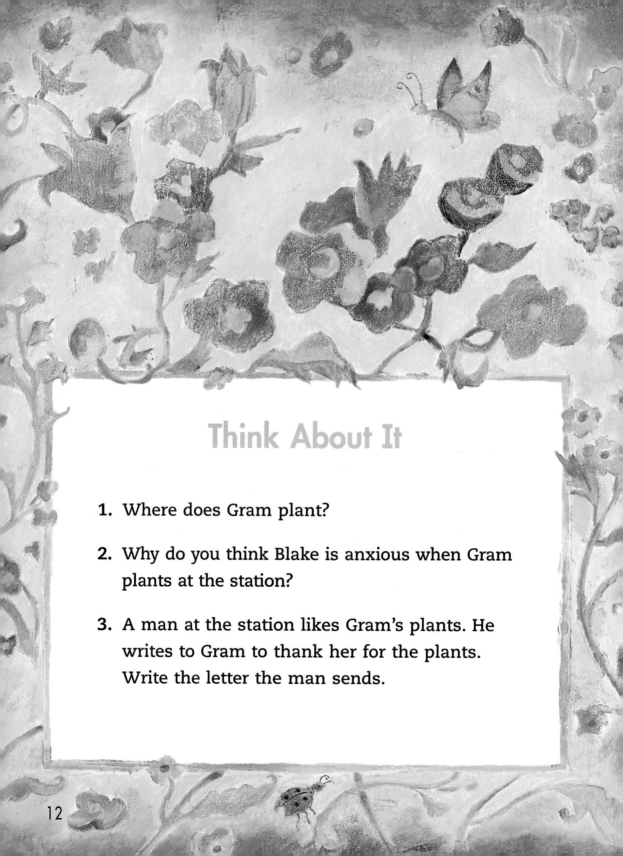

Think About It

1. Where does Gram plant?

2. Why do you think Blake is anxious when Gram plants at the station?

3. A man at the station likes Gram's plants. He writes to Gram to thank her for the plants. Write the letter the man sends.

Blooming Riddles

Carnation

What flower acts silly?

What flowers have the same
name as a part of your face?

What flower names a big cat that's
just fine?

Which flower is married to a mommy?

What flower would be a good name
for a country full of automobiles?

Which flower scared the fairy-tale
monster?

Poppy

Tulip

Dandelion

Snap dragon

Daffodil

Answers: daffy-dil, tu-lips,
dandy-lion, poppy, car-nation,
snap-dragon

13

CLICK!

by Celeste Albright illustrated by Michele Noiset

All the kids in our class like Miss Wise. She makes us smile!

"Look at this pin that Kim gave me!" Miss Wise says. "Isn't it a kick?" She has the pin on her hat. It's a fish pin, and the fish has big pink lips.

Mike Briggs says, "Smile, Miss Wise!"

Miss Wise grins.

That's Mike for you. Click, click, click, all the time.

"I collect pins," Miss Wise says. "Collecting them is what I do in my leisure time. It can have its disappointments, when I can't get the pin I want. The solution is perseverance!

"See if you like being collectors, kids. Bring a collection to class when you can."

Mike visits Tim to see what he's collecting.

"I have nine hats," Tim says. He has on six of them. "Is this a collection?"

"It looks like a collection to me," Mike says.

"Mike, what will you do for a collection?" Tim asks.

"It's not a problem," says Mike. "You'll see. Smile!"

Mike rides off on his bike to see Jill.

"I'm a stamp collector," says Jill. "I like sitting and looking at my stamps."

"That white one with the plane is my favorite," Mike says.

Jill picks it up.

"Smile, Jill!" says Mike.

CLICK!

Then Mike bikes over to Linda's.
"I collect pigs!" says Linda.
"Pigs?" Mike looks uneasy.
"Don't they stink a bit? Do your
neighbors get mad? You could
compromise with them and collect
cats. Cats would be no problem."

Linda chortles. "My pigs are no
problem to our neighbors." She
invites Mike in to see them.

Linda has pigs of all sizes. Many were gifts. She has ticking pigs, big pigs, and five pink pigs.

Linda picks up her favorite, a pig in a hat and wig.

"What do you collect, Mike?" she asks.

Mike grins. He says, "You'll see in class. Smile, Miss Pig in a Wig!"

CLICK!

19

"What's in there, Mike?" the kids ask.

"You are!" Mike says. "Take a look!" There's Tim in his hats. There are Jill and Linda. All the kids are there.

"That's quite a collection!" Miss Wise says. "A smile collection! I like it. Now, you smile, Mike!"

And what a fine smile it is.

Think About It

1. What does Mike collect? How does he collect them?

2. Why do you think Miss Wise asks her class to be collectors?

3. Write a news story about the collections made by the kids in Miss Wise's class.

A Troublesome NOSE

by Linda Lott   illustrated by Russ Wilson

Miss Jones's class is planning a holiday pageant. Ron is glad that they are going to act out his favorite book.

In the book, a fox, a dog, and a frog make a visit to a tropical land. They plan a fine holiday, but troublesome problems come up.

Ron is restless. He hopes to get a role, and he is not disappointed. He gets to be the fox. He has the greatest lines—they're all jokes. All the kids like the fox.

Ron says his lines over and over so he will not make a mistake on stage. His mom and dad will be coming to the pageant.

The time comes for the dress rehearsal, and Miss Jones gives out the costumes. Ron's is a fake fox nose.

The long nose looks fine, but it's a troublesome nose. The problem is that it flip-flops up and down. It flips up, and Ron can't see. It flops down, and it's over his lips. When Ron says his lines, all that comes out is "Mmm, mmm, mmm." The kids can't get the jokes.

Ron jogs home, swinging the nose on its string. When he gets inside, Mom looks up.

"What a fine nose!" she says.

"It's not fine at all," Ron says. He pops the nose on and says his lines. The nose flip-flops up and down. Mom can't get anything but "Mmm, mmm, mmm."

Dad grins and hands Ron some tape. "You'll have to fix it so it doesn't flip-flop," he says.

"I hope I can fix it in time," Ron says.

At the pageant, it's time for the fox to be seen. Ron lopes onto the stage. All the kids smile.

Mom and Dad gaze attentively at the nose. What if it still slips? Can Ron cope with it?

The nose does slip! First it rides up so Ron can't see. Ron gropes for it, and the kids all grin. Then the nose slips down over Ron's lips.

"Mmm, mmm, mmm," says the fox.

The kids are having a fit. Ron grins back at them. Then he puts the nose up on top. Now he can say his lines just fine. He does not make one mistake.

Mom and Dad clap and clap. Then they make a visit to the stage.

"Good job, Ron!" they say. "You came up with a fine solution to your problem."

"I like that fox role," says Ron. "The jokes are all good ones. The troublesome nose was the greatest joke of all!"

Think About It

1. What is Ron's role in the holiday pageant? Why does he like that role?

2. Why is the big nose the greatest joke of all?

3. After the play, Ron writes a postcard to his friend. He tells all about the troublesome nose. Write the postcard Ron sends.

The Nose Knows

Noses show up in a lot of expressions. Do you know what these mean?

Tom won the election **by a nose.**

Your guess was right **on the nose.**

My uncle had to **pay through the nose** for his fancy
   new car.

Don't **turn up your nose** at a hot
   breakfast!

Noses have even been the subject of
rhymes, such as this limerick. Do you know
any other rhymes about noses?

My friend's a small critter named Rose
With a star on the end of her nose.
   I agree that she's not
   Such a good-looking tot,
But she's cute for a mole, I suppose.

Joe DiMaggio

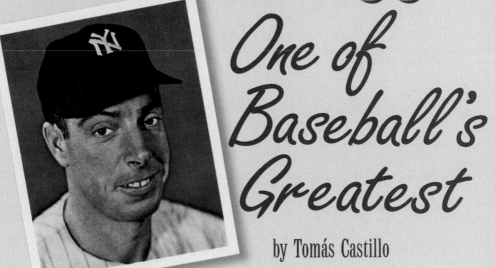

One of Baseball's Greatest

by Tomás Castillo

Joe DiMaggio, the son of immigrant parents, began his baseball career in 1936. He came to the New York Yankees when Lou Gehrig was with them. DiMaggio was 21 and glad to make such a fine team.

The Yankees' manager had hopes for DiMaggio, but Yankees fans were upset. The new man had a bad leg. People asked, "Can he run around the bases? Can he hit in Yankee Stadium?"

In no time, people got to like DiMaggio. They came to the stadium to see him. He was modest, but his hitting was making him a favorite of Yankees fans. Baseball fans from all over agreed that Joe DiMaggio was a tremendous find.

DiMaggio got 206 hits in 1936, and 29 of them were home runs! The Yankees' manager noted that DiMaggio was valuable to the team, and his salary went up.

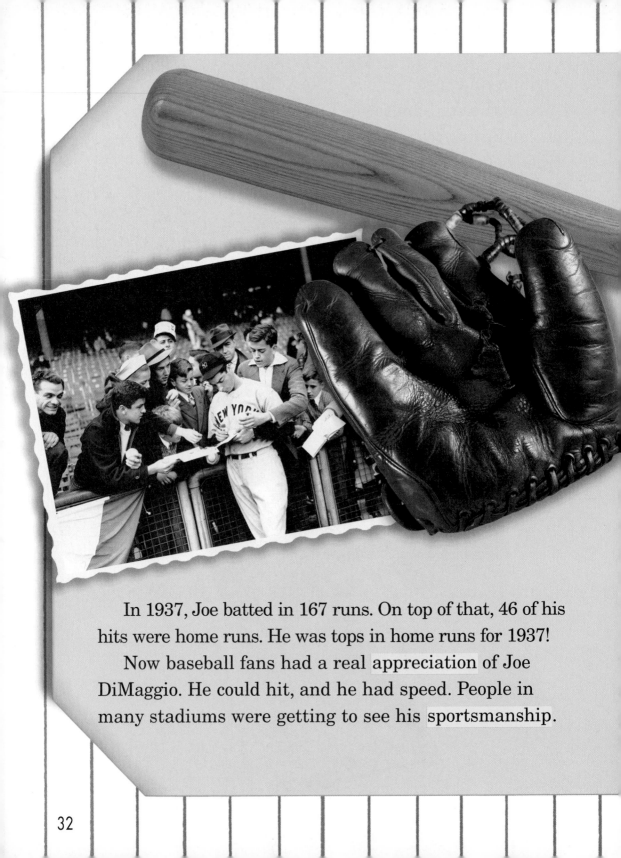

In 1937, Joe batted in 167 runs. On top of that, 46 of his hits were home runs. He was tops in home runs for 1937!

Now baseball fans had a real appreciation of Joe DiMaggio. He could hit, and he had speed. People in many stadiums were getting to see his sportsmanship.

DiMaggio still had a "hot bat" in 1938 and 1939. His home runs went down, but his batting went up. In 1939, it was the best in all of baseball.

In 1940, his batting fell off a little. The Yankees slid out of their top spot. The upset manager of the Yankees had to hope his team could be tops again in 1941.

FINAL

DAILY ● NEWS

NEW YORK'S PICTURE NEWSPAPER

Vol. 17. No. 268   48 Pages   New York, Monday, May 4, 1936   2 Cents

DIMAGGIO SMACKS 3 HITS IN DEBUT; YANKS WIN, 14-5

Story on Page 42

The Yankees did win back the top spot, but Joe DiMaggio outdid his team. On May 15, 1941, in a game with the Chicago White Sox, he began an amazing hitting streak. First he got at least one hit in each of ten games in a row. Then it was 20 games. When was Joe DiMaggio going to stop getting hits?

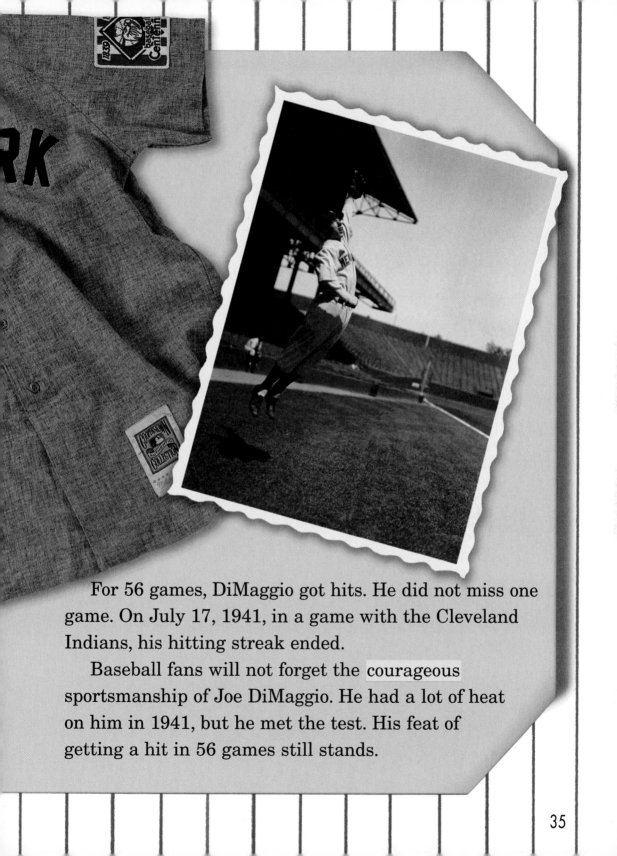

For 56 games, DiMaggio got hits. He did not miss one game. On July 17, 1941, in a game with the Cleveland Indians, his hitting streak ended.

Baseball fans will not forget the courageous sportsmanship of Joe DiMaggio. He had a lot of heat on him in 1941, but he met the test. His feat of getting a hit in 56 games still stands.

JOSEPH PAUL DI MAGGIO
NEW YORK A.L. 1936 TO 1951

HIT SAFELY IN 56 CONSECUTIVE GAMES
FOR MAJOR LEAGUE RECORD 1941. HIT 2
HOME-RUNS IN ONE INNING 1936. HIT 3
HOME-RUNS IN ONE GAME (3 TIMES). HOLDS
NUMEROUS BATTING RECORDS. PLAYED IN
10 WORLD SERIES (51 GAMES) AND 11 ALL
STAR GAMES. MOST VALUABLE PLAYER
A.L. 1939, 1941, 1947.

Joe DiMaggio retired from baseball in 1951. The Yankees were sad to see him go. So were baseball fans from New York and all over. In 1955, he was voted into the Baseball Hall of Fame.

DiMaggio had a fine life. He was 84 when it ended on March 8, 1999. He had given a lot to the game he cared about. Baseball fans will not forget Joe DiMaggio. He was one of the greatest.

Think About It

1. Why was Joe DiMaggio voted into the Baseball Hall of Fame?

2. Why did the fans like Joe DiMaggio?

3. Suppose you were in the stands when Joe DiMaggio got a hit in his amazing hitting streak. At home, you wanted to tell about the game in your diary. Write your diary entry.

Amelia's Flying Lesson

by Celeste Albright
illustrated by Stacey Schuett

"Amelia! What are you doing out there in the dark?"

"Just looking," said Amelia. "What a sky! There's not a single cloud up there."

"So what?" said June. "It's nighttime. It's too dark to see anything."

"No, it's not. It's a starstruck night out here. Come and see for yourself!"

"Not me!" June said. Then, thinking it over, she went out and sat with her friend.

June and Amelia were not at all alike. Amelia was outspoken. June was quiet. June enjoyed elegant dresses with ribbons. Amelia liked practical pants with pockets. June had fun with her miniature tea set. Amelia just dreamed of flying.

But June liked Amelia, and Amelia enjoyed being with June. They were pals, and that was that.

The next day was brisk. The fresh breeze gave Amelia an idea. She pulled wood planks to the backyard.

"I *will* fly up in that sky someday," she said to June. "When I look down, I'll see the tops of clouds."

"Not me!" June said. She marveled at how brave Amelia was.

A plank flew past June and landed with a plunk.

"Amelia! What's all this stuff for?" she asked.

"We're going to make a slide," Amelia said. "We'll go so fast! You'll see — it will feel just like flying."

"Not me!" said June. "You can slide if you want to, but I'll just watch."

"Take the end of this tape," Amelia said. "What's the elevation of this shed?"

Amelia stuck to the job, and June enjoyed helping. At last they got the slide up. Then Amelia tugged an apple box out of the shed. She put wheels on it and lined it with a dark red rug.

"Let's go," she said.

"Not me! And not you!" June said, tugging at Amelia's sleeve. "You'll get hurt!"

Amelia just grinned and went to the top of the slide. She jumped into the box.

Rumble, creak, rattle, clunk!

The apple box flew down the slide! At the bottom, the wheels stuck in the mud. Amelia landed with a thump.

"Amelia! Amelia!" June called.

Amelia jumped up and looked at the sky. She grinned at June.

"That was fun!" she said.

June grinned back. "Now it's my turn!" she said. "You flew down that slide, Amelia! Now I want to fly, too!"

Think About It

1. What did Amelia and June make?

2. Why is "Amelia's Flying Lesson" a good title for this story?

3. What do you think will happen when June goes down the slide? Write the next part of the story.

Can-Do Kid

by Kaye Gager
illustrated by
Jeremy Tugeau

CHARACTERS:

WALT, 12 years old

DUNCAN, Walt's
  friend, also
  12 years old

MAN at CD stall
People shopping

SETTING:

Stalls set up
outside a stadium to
sell new and old things.

WALT: Let's go look at the CD stall. There it
is, over in the middle.

DUNCAN: We went to that stall last time, Walt! You
spent all your money there! I want to check out the
sunglasses on that rack.

WALT: I just want to see if they have any Hot Rock CDs.

DUNCAN: OK, OK. We can just look. (*Walt and Duncan walk over to the CD stall.*)

CD MAN: Hello, kids! What can I do for you?

WALT: Do you have the first Hot Rock CD?

CD MAN: I do indeed! It's one of their best! (*He hands Walt a CD.*)

WALT (*looking at the CD in the palm of his hand*): No! It can't be ten bucks!

CD MAN (*indignantly*): I run an honest business here! Hot Rock
is big now. All their CDs cost ten bucks.

WALT (*shamefacedly*): All I have is five bucks. I can't afford it.

CD MAN: Too bad. You look like an honest kid. Not like those
shiftless ones who hang out here. Could you get the rest of
the money? I can keep this CD for you until two.

WALT: OK! I can do it. I'll get it by then.

DUNCAN: How can you do it? You think five bucks is going to fall from the sky?

WALT: Calm down, will you? I can earn it.

DUNCAN: Give it up, Walt. CDs are just a luxury, and you have lots.

WALT: No, Duncan! Giving up is no good. (*He stands next to the CD stall and sets out his hat.*)

DUNCAN: What are you going to do? Sing?

WALT: You've got it!

DUNCAN: Nonsense! You can't sing.

WALT: I've picked up a thing or two from
my CD collection. You'll see! (*He sings* ad lib:)
"If you want to talk the talk,
You've got to walk the walk.
If you want to be a man,
You've got to do what you can . . ."
(*A lot of people stop. They clap and put money
in the hat. Then they visit the CD stall.*)

WALT (*elated*): See that? I earned six bucks! Now I can afford that CD!

CD MAN: Kid, you're good for business! Do you have tapes of your songs? Would you give me the privilege of selling them?

WALT (*nodding assent*): I'll make some and bring them next week.

DUNCAN (*shaking his head*): No nonsense, man. You can sing!

CD MAN: You can do what you say you will, too. I'd call you a real can-do kid!

Think About It

1. What problem does Walt have? How does he solve it?

2. What are some adjectives that could tell what Walt is like? How do you know he is like that?

3. List three other ways Walt could have earned the money he needed.

How Silly!

Q: Why did the cat buy some CDs at the mall?
A: She liked mew-sic.

Q: What did all the band members order for lunch?
A: Tune-a-fish sandwiches.

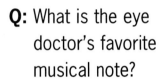

Q: What is the eye doctor's favorite musical note?
A: C-sharp.

Q: What is the geologist's favorite type of music?
A: Rock.

Q: What do you call someone who sings while putting fancy paper on packages?
A: A rapper.

SMALL BUT BRAVE

by Susan McCloskey
illustrated by Sachiko Yoshikawa

Loyal was a small black-and-white dog. He lived in a good home with his friend, Ray. Loyal was always by Ray's side. He was a loyal friend.

Loyal had a heavy gray blanket to sleep on. He had a green dish to eat from. He played with the ants and snails in the grass outside. Every day he and Ray waited on the stairs for the mail. Then off they went for a walk, rain or shine.

Loyal liked to chase things, but he would not hurt them. He was not cruel.

One day he chased a little bug, a fat frog, and a happy robin. The bug scuttled away. The frog hopped away. The robin sang and then flitted away.

Ray patted Loyal's back. "You are small but brave!" he said. Loyal wagged his tail. He felt so important!

Home of LOYAL,
SMALL BUT BRAVE

That night Ray twined a string through the gate. He was hanging a present for Loyal. It was a name plate that said "Home of Loyal, Small but Brave."

Ray's praise made Loyal want to be the bravest dog in the world. To find out if he was the bravest, he would have to leave home. He stretched out on his blanket and began plotting how to do this.

The next night, Ray neglected to close the gate. Loyal sailed out and was off down the street. He ran and ran a very long way. At last he stopped to rest.

A big dog on a chain laughed at him. "You are small and insignificant!" he said. The dog did not look cruel, so Loyal was not afraid.

"I am small but brave!" he said.

A man named Frank came out. Frank was impressed with Loyal and gave him some important jobs. One of these was to keep the fox from getting the hens. It was the loneliest job of all.

Sometimes Loyal didn't sleep all night. He kept trotting around and around the pen encircling the hens.

One night the fox *did* make a raid. Loyal raised a
fuss, hoping the fox would run off. He was surprised
when it grabbed his leg in a steely grip. But Loyal
was unyielding, and at last the fox ran away.

Loyal lay in a pile of hay. He was sad and in
pain. He said, "I am small and brave, but I miss Ray.
I miss my home and my heavy gray blanket. I am
the loneliest dog in the world!"

Loyal got up and limped home to Ray. Ray fixed up his leg and said, "Loyal, you are small but brave. In fact, you are the bravest dog in the world!" Loyal felt good again. He stretched out on his blanket and fell fast asleep.

Sometimes Loyal thinks of his battle with the fox. Then he lays his nose on Ray's lap. He knows it's important to be brave, but it's better to have a best friend.

Think About It

1. How does Loyal prove that he is brave?

2. How does Ray feel about Loyal? How do you know?

3. Loyal thinks having a best friend is more important than being brave. Do you agree? Write your reasons.

Bringing Back the
PUFFINS

by Caren B. Stelson
illustrated by Paul Mirocha

Spring has come back to Egg Rock, but will the puffins come back too? A man named Steve Kress watches and hopes. For a long time, no puffins had nested on these uninhabited rocks. Then Kress started a plan to bring them back. He hopes his puffin plan will go right.

Over 100 years ago, puffins nested on Egg Rock. Kress wanted to see them there again. In 1973, he and his team went to a land that has many puffins. They collected puffin chicks, being very careful with them, and then rushed them back to Egg Rock.

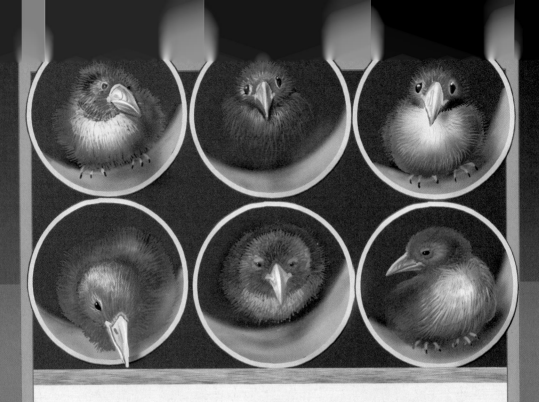

Steve Kress and his team acted as parents to tend the puffin chicks. They made a village of burrows for the chicks to nestle in. They fed them fresh fish and kept them safe from dangers, such as gulls. Kress and his team made good puffin parents!

One night the puffins came out of their village of burrows. It was time for them to venture into the sea. Each made a wobbling flight, splashed in, and went out into the dark night.

Would the puffins come back to breed and to tend their chicks? Kress hoped that in two to three years, they would instinctively do this.

There are many dangers for puffins at sea. They can be eaten if a gull spies them. They can be stranded in fishing nets. They can be harmed by big waves.

Yet puffins are made for sea life. They can dive deep and swim fast. They use their wings to swim and their webbed feet to steer. They catch fish with their sharp beaks. Kress hoped at least some of his puffins would make it back to Egg Rock.

Now Steve Kress sits on Egg Rock, keeping watch and hoping his plan was not just a dream. He watches for a long, long time.

Then Kress spies a black speck in flight. The speck gets bigger and bigger as it sweeps over the sea. Kress leaps to his feet and yells to his team. The puffins have come back to Egg Rock!

Think About It

1. How did Steve Kress and his team help puffin chicks live on Egg Rock?

2. Why did the adult puffins come back to Egg Rock?

3. What else do you want to know about puffins? Write three questions you would like to ask Steve Kress.

Winging It

There once was a small, chubby puffin
Whose favorite food was a muffin.
   No fish could she catch,
   No eggs could she hatch,
For her beak she forever was stuffin'.

While strolling along down
   the path,
I met with a pelican's wrath.
   "Dear sir!" cried the bird.
   "I am shocked! It's absurd
To walk in on a bird in his bath!"

Green Tomatoes

by Charlene Norman

illustrated by Liz Conrad

Martin skidded his bike to a stop, making a haze of dust. "Here's Mom's list," he said to Nick. "Can I feed the carp in your pond?"

Nick smiled as he filled a sack with tomatoes, carrots, and beans. "Now you can go feed the carp."

Martin ran to the backyard. "You have the greatest garden!" he called.

Carla and Lil got what they needed from Nick's stand. "We're making pickles," said Carla.

"I like pickles," Nick said, "if they're a little sweet."

"I like frogs," said Lil. "They're green."

"We have some in the pond. Go visit them if you like," Nick said.

Miss Marlene gave Nick some money for tomatoes. "May I sit on your garden seat for a while?" she asked. "I like to inhale the sweet smells there."

Nick smiled and agreed. This was the season for garden visits.

In the afternoon, Nick did some of his favorite things in his garden. He measured neat lines for the next part of his garden mural. He fed the carp in his backyard pond. He trimmed the lavender and the trumpet vines by the seat in the corner. He weeded the bed of beans.

Then he stopped. "Who stole the tomatoes off my plants?" he yelled. "They were still small and green—they were for my next big harvest!"

Did one of his neighbors pick them? Then Nick saw a line of lavender petals leaving the garden. He decided to track them.

The petals led Nick to Carla and Lil's yard. Carla was sitting on the steps, reading. Lil was swinging a plastic bat.

"Help!" he called. "My green tomatoes are missing from my tomato bed. Have you seen them?"

"I haven't seen them," said Carla, "but I'll help you look." They looked in Lil's wagon and sandbox, but there were no tomatoes.

Then Carla saw Lil hit a green ball. "Lil has lots of small plastic balls, but no green ones!" she said. Carla and Nick ran over. They grabbed small green tomatoes out of Lil's box.

"Mine!" yelled Lil. "I like the green ones best!"

Nick held up a tomato. "I can't sell this. It's too green. It's useless." He sniffed and blinked.

Carla looked down. She felt bad. "I didn't see Lil taking your tomatoes," she said. "I'll give you the money for them."

"No," said Nick. "I can't take money for green tomatoes."

After a week, Carla and Lil came to Nick's stand, grinning. They gave Nick a jar of pickled green tomatoes.

Nick bit into one. "This isn't useless. This is quite a treat!" He gave Carla a wide grin. "I know I can sell these!"

Then Nick patted Lil's back. "Next year, you can help me harvest more green tomatoes to pickle. But not all of them!"

Think About It

1. Why do Carla and Lil give Nick a jar of pickled green tomatoes?

2. Why won't Nick and Lil harvest *all* the green tomatoes for pickles next year?

3. Next year Nick will make a poster to tell his neighbors that it is harvest time. Make a poster that Nick could use.

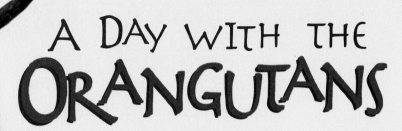

A DAY WITH THE ORANGUTANS

by Jeannie W. Berger

You are alone in the rain forest of Borneo, far from any road. The forest is thick, green, and overgrown with vines. Bugs buzz in your ears as you keep looking, looking. Then you hear a tree shake and you stop in your tracks. When you look up, something looks down at you. Is it what you think? Yes, you're in luck! You've found what you were looking for.

It's a baby orangutan! Baby orangutans are endangered. Some are smuggled out of the forest for sale as pets. Some become orphans when people catch and sell their moms. When trees are cut down, all orangutans are in danger. At least this baby orangutan is not one of the rain forest orphans.

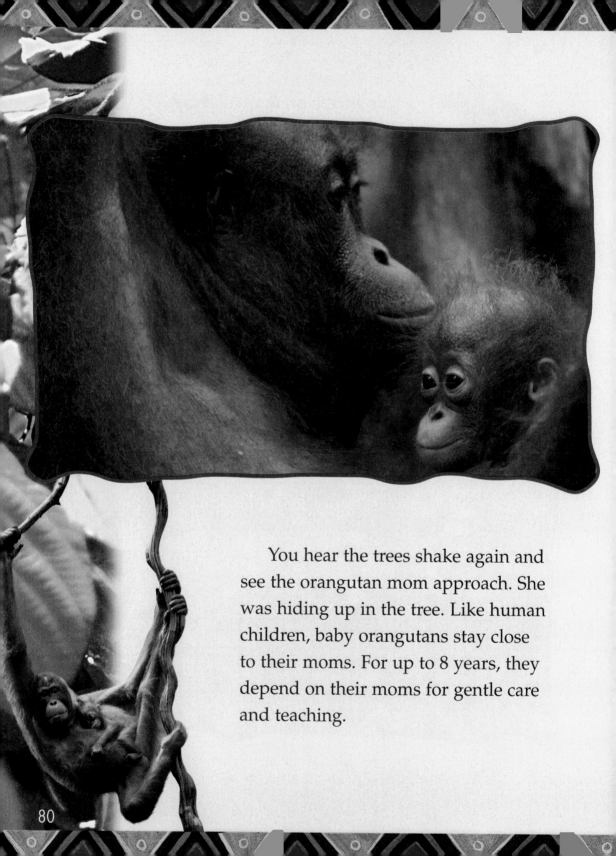

You hear the trees shake again and see the orangutan mom approach. She was hiding up in the tree. Like human children, baby orangutans stay close to their moms. For up to 8 years, they depend on their moms for gentle care and teaching.

Do not coax the baby orangutan to come to you. It is known that orangutans like to be left alone. The baby you see seems content. When a baby orangutan is jealous, it shows its displeasure using facial expressions. When it is very upset, it may throw a tantrum, just as a human baby does. Even orangutan moms have to deal with bad behavior!

If you can, take a good look at the
orangutan's hands and feet. They are just
right for gripping tree branches. The baby
orangutans must practice swinging from
branch to branch. This kind of play helps
them develop good coordination. They will
depend on this to be safe in the treetops.

The orangutan mom teaches her baby behaviors it will need when it is grown. Each evening, she shows it how to make a nest in a tree. She makes the nest just big enough for them to sleep in. In time, her baby will practice making a nest of its own. For now, this baby is glad to sleep with its mom.

The day is slipping away, and it's time to go back to your camp. You have a lot to think about after watching the orangutans roaming free. You now understand why some people want to save the rain forest of Borneo. It is an expression of caring for the orangutans who make it their home.

Think About It

1. What is life like for a baby orangutan?

2. This selection is written as if the reader is in the rain forest. Why do you think the author wrote it that way?

3. Imagine you have gone to Borneo to see the orangutans. Write to a friend, telling what you are thinking, doing, and feeling.

A HOME
ON THE
OREGON TRAIL

by
Sydnie Meltzer Kleinhenz
illustrations by
Ande Cook

Kate felt lonely as she brushed crumbles of sod from her pink conch shell. She missed the sea it had come from and her old home in Baltimore. She had loved visiting with neighbors on her front porch there.

The sod dwelling felt almost like home now. The quilts Kate and her mother had hung over the sod added color to the drab walls. Outside, the rippling waves of grass almost substituted for the splashing waves near Baltimore.

Jed ran in. "Kate," he called. "I've got more kindling for our fire. I've got something else, too—a traveling man who needs a meal."

"We welcome all travelers on the Oregon Trail," Kate said, smiling. "Come in! No one has visited us in a long time."

"Thank you," the man said. He didn't look very old—maybe 20, Kate guessed. "I'm Patrick Guthrey. I take pictures."

Kate's mother and father came in from the fields. They were very pleased to meet Patrick.

At dinner, Patrick told the family many tales of his travels on the Oregon Trail. Then he invited them to pose outside for a portrait. Mother and daughter wore their best bonnets. Kate also wore a big smile for Patrick!

Back inside, they looked at Patrick's prints. His landscapes were splendid.

A rustle distracted them. They looked up as a king snake slid through the sod above one of the quilts! Patrick tossed it outside.

When he came back in, he looked alarmed. "Friends, that glow outside is not sunset. It's a grass fire!"

The two men rushed to beat back the flames. Jed drove the mule and goat to the sod barn. Mother and daughter ran to chase in the hens and gather up the chicks.

Then everyone huddled in the sod home. A wall of fire roared through the windbreak and scorched the paddock. After it had blazed on past the sod dwelling, they stepped outside to look around.

The sea of grass rippled no more. All was smoking blackness. "Thank goodness we're all safe!" Kate's mother exclaimed.

"At least there's time to plant again," said her father. "We'll still get a harvest."

"I'll help you in the fields before I travel on," Patrick said.

Kate's father gave Patrick's hand a shake. "Thank you," he said. "Will you come back in the fall to share our harvest?"

"Of course," said Patrick, smiling at Kate. "I'll have to bring you your portrait."

Kate smiled back at Patrick. She was thinking that she would not be lonely on the plains anymore. It had not been a perfect day, but it had been a perfect visit!

Think About It

1. Why does Patrick go to Kate's home?

2. Why was the family happy to have a visitor?

3. Write a list of words that tell about Kate at the beginning. Write another list of words that tell about Kate at the end. Then use your lists to write a paragraph about Kate. Tell how and why she changes.

Way Out West

Gather round, young 'uns, and I'll tell you a tale
Of Great-grandpappy on the Oregon Trail.
Great-grandpappy—his name was Mort—
Wrestled wild animals just for sport.

Month after month Mort's wagon creaked on.
It seemed his group never would reach Oregon.
Day after day that desert stayed dry.
The oxen and the people were just about to fry.

"Hey, Mort," the boss yelled. "I'm givin' you a chore.
Your job's to make it rain! I want to see it pour!"
Well, Mort, he didn't know just what to do.
He was sharp, but making rain was new.

So he sat on the floor of his wagon for a bit.
He pondered and he thought, then he cried, "That's it!"
That evenin' in the woods, he found a hungry bear.
Then he teased it and he ran. Mort could run like a hare!

Up the tallest peak, feet churnin' like wheels,
Flew Mort with that bear hot on his heels.
He stopped at the top, and the bear rushed by.
Off flew that bear, right into the sky!

Its claws ripped the sky. Wide open it tore!
Then down came the rain, and did it pour!
Now all of you know the daring tale
Of Great-grandpappy on the Oregon Trail.

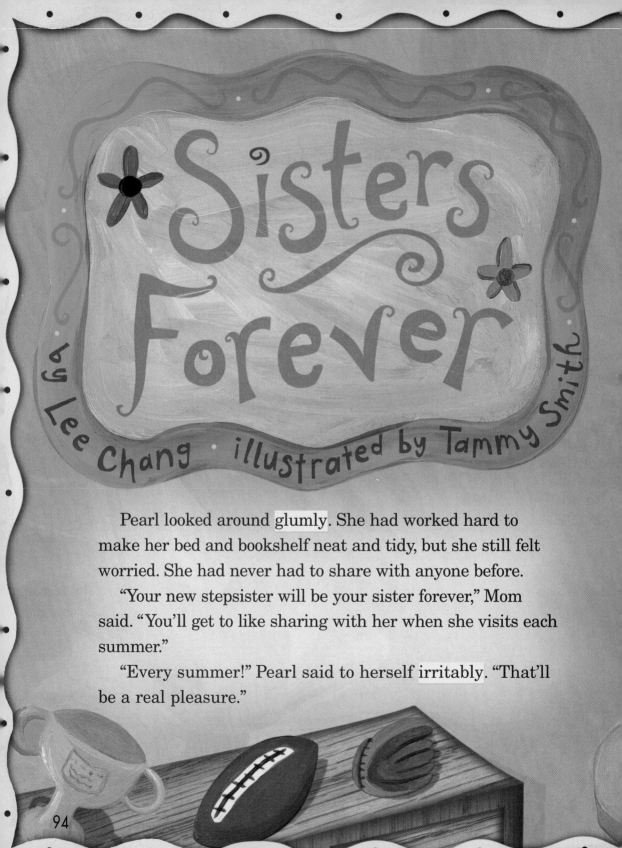

Sisters Forever

by Lee Chang • illustrated by Tammy Smith

Pearl looked around glumly. She had worked hard to make her bed and bookshelf neat and tidy, but she still felt worried. She had never had to share with anyone before.

"Your new stepsister will be your sister forever," Mom said. "You'll get to like sharing with her when she visits each summer."

"Every summer!" Pearl said to herself irritably. "That'll be a real pleasure."

94

All the way to the airport to meet LaVerne's plane, Pearl tried to ignore the situation. She was just getting used to having a stepfather, and now she had to get used to having a stepsister, too.

When LaVerne walked off the plane, Pearl gave her a weak smile. LaVerne wore her curly hair long with a bow. Pearl kept her hair short for sports. LaVerne looked like a girl with very different interests from hers. How would the two of them ever get along?

Pearl did not feel more hopeful when her stepsister unpacked her things. First LaVerne put a stuffed toy cat next to Pearl's baseball mitt. Then she cluttered the tidy shelf with her books and the rest of her possessions.

Pearl's disposition changed. She didn't feel happy anymore. She felt that LaVerne was imposing on her. Pearl didn't want to be mean, but she couldn't help feeling a grudge.

LaVerne seemed no happier with the situation than Pearl. At dinner, the girls started to bicker. They both looked angry and sad.

Pearl's stepfather tried to cheer them up. "This summer will be fun," he said. "I like having my two girls together. I wouldn't be surprised if you find you like some of the same pastimes."

The girls just frowned and looked down at their plates. They had to be sisters forever, but they didn't have to like it.

The next morning Pearl got up early while LaVerne was still sleeping. She glared at LaVerne and her possessions, and then she sneaked out. Her parents would want her to take LaVerne to meet her friends. Pearl had no such plans. She ate quickly and left, intending to ignore LaVerne.

Pearl played soccer with her friends all morning. At lunchtime she went home feeling bad. Sneaking out on LaVerne had been mean. Now Mom might make her stay home all afternoon and play with LaVerne and her stuffed toys.

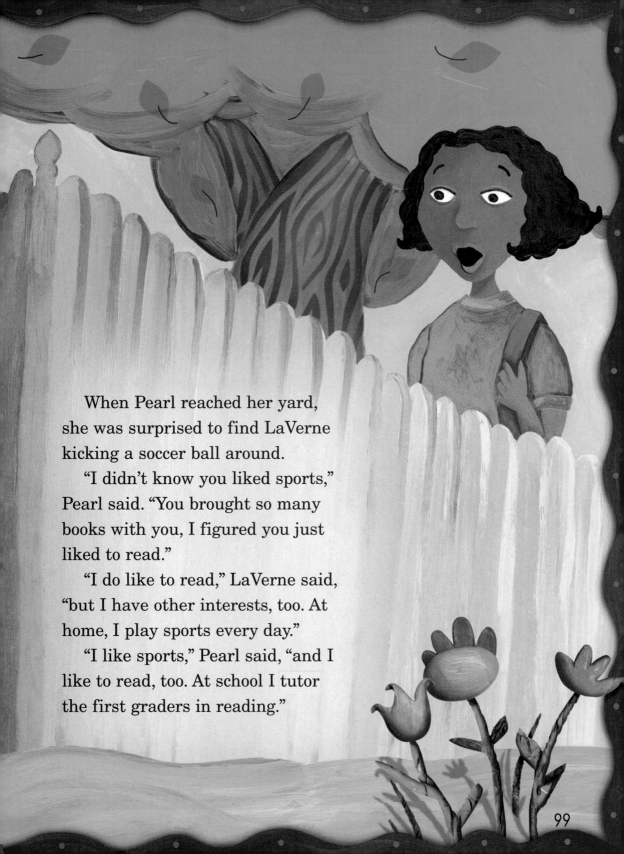

When Pearl reached her yard, she was surprised to find LaVerne kicking a soccer ball around.

"I didn't know you liked sports," Pearl said. "You brought so many books with you, I figured you just liked to read."

"I do like to read," LaVerne said, "but I have other interests, too. At home, I play sports every day."

"I like sports," Pearl said, "and I like to read, too. At school I tutor the first graders in reading."

"You can read my books if you want to," said LaVerne. "Do you like to play board games?"

"Yes, I do," said Pearl. "I guess your dad was right. We *do* have some pastimes we both like."

"I guess parents can be right once in a while," LaVerne joked, and they both laughed.

For the first time, the girls gave each other a real smile. The situation was not so bad after all. It began to look as if being sisters forever *could* turn out to be a real pleasure.

Think About It

1. Why does Pearl have to share with LaVerne?

2. Why does Pearl think LaVerne doesn't like sports?

3. Think about Pearl and LaVerne. Write one paragraph telling how the two girls are the same. Write another paragraph telling how they are different.

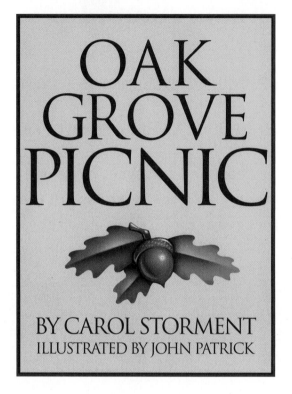

OAK GROVE PICNIC

BY CAROL STORMENT
ILLUSTRATED BY JOHN PATRICK

The word was out, and before midday the news was all over the field. Everyone had been waiting all summer for this day.

Ruben, a squirrel, heard the news first. He scampered over to see his neighbor, a wood rat named Bo. Bo had been making the acquaintance of several more wood rats. Now, they were all exploring a jumble of dry grass and clover, scrounging for something to eat.

"Guess what!" Ruben called out. "The acorns are ready! It's time to get over to the oak grove."

Bo looked up. "How do you know?" he asked. "It's so hot, I wouldn't want to go all the way over there for nothing."

"I heard the treehoppers talking this morning," said Ruben.

"You mean you were eavesdropping!" Bo said with a laugh. "Why do you believe those insects? What do they know about acorns?"

"They have a talent for finding things to eat," Ruben said. "You know there isn't a bite to be had around here."

"Oh, all right," Bo said. "Let's go before the acorns are all eaten up."

From above, Davis the jay heard the wood rat and the squirrel fussing. Flying quickly, he returned to his nest.

"Hi-ho! It's picnic day in the oak grove!" he shouted to Mavis. "Wake up before our winter's stores are taken from us!"

Mavis looked at him sleepily. "It's too hot to go exploring today," she said, refusing to move.

That sent Davis hopping and flapping around the nest. His antics were familiar to Mavis. Davis was a rather excitable bird.

"Do you want to let those wood rats and squirrels get there first?" Davis's screech was anything but musical, as singing was not one of his talents.

His words, however, were enough to get Mavis up. The two jays set off, keeping a sharp eye out for owls.

The owls could not miss such a racket.
However, they had bigger plans for lunch than
two skinny jays. They knew there would be a full
menu of animals at the picnic! They followed Mavis
and Davis across the familiar fields.

Iris the deer and her baby, Amy, were grazing in a
vacant clearing. Little Amy looked up wistfully at the
musical jumble of birds gliding over, wishing she could fly.

"I wish we had wings, Mommy," she said sadly. "Then
maybe we could find some new green leaves to eat."

Smiling sympathetically, her mother said, "I know you're hungry, Amy. It's the end of summer, so it's logical that everything is dry. When it's picnic day, we'll have . . ."

"I know, I know," Amy said. "The moment the acorns start falling from the oak trees, we can go eat all we want."

Iris told Amy, "The acorns are a treat, but they're more than that. At the end of the dry season, they help us all get fat for winter. Everyone around here will use something from the oaks. Some will save and hide the acorns for the future, and some will eat the leaves. Others will make homes from the twigs. Many of us would not be able to make it through the winter without the oaks."

Amy saw birds, squirrels, and wood rats rushing by. "Mommy, look around! I think it's happening right now!"

Picnic day in the oak grove was indeed in full swing. Bugs were munching leaves. Squirrels and jays were arguing over jumbles of ripe acorns. Everyone ate and ate, while keeping one eye on the owls.

The owls finally had to give up on lunch. They were not used to being awake in the daytime, and they became very sleepy. When the owls went home to nap, everyone else relaxed. Picnic day ended with a lot of buzzing and humming and snoring in the shade under the oak trees.

Think About It

1. What is picnic day in the oak grove? At what time of year does it happen?

2. Why is picnic day so important to the animals?

3. Two children sit quietly behind a bush and watch the animals at the picnic. What do they see? What do they think about the picnic? Write your ideas.

Critter Definitions

katydid: the answer to the question, "Who ate the cookie from the cookie jar?"

worm: the opposite of *cool*

hornet: a small musical instrument that you blow into

deer: quite a sweetie

gull: not a boy

cheetah: somebody who doesn't play by the rules

RABBIT!

rabbit: the sound made by a frog

parakeets: a set of two keets

A Pen Pal in Vietnam

by Pam Zollman   illustrated by Winson Trang

Dear Kim,

I was so happy to get your first letter. My neighbor will be our interpreter. She tells me that you are nine and that your home is on a farm in Vietnam.

I'm nine, too. My home is in a small village in California. I've seen pictures of people in straw hats planting rice in Vietnam. Do you grow rice on your farm?

Write soon,

Michelle

Rice is a major crop in Vietnam. These women are wearing traditional bamboo hats.

Hello, Kim!

I'm picturing you helping with the rice crop. I guess the irrigation makes the fields muddy to walk in. Our lake has a muddy bottom. I don't like walking in mud—do you?

I eat rice occasionally, but I don't like it much. If I had to eat it at every meal, it might overwhelm me! Then again, I might get to like it!

I'm glad you can pronounce my name. I'm eager to hear about your canoe trip to the city. I was in a rowboat one time. Would your canoe be the equivalent of a rowboat?

Write soon,

Michelle

Dear Kim,

I'm sorry this letter is so late. My little sister hid your letter. She gets into a lot of mischief, but this mischief wasn't fun for me. I hope she won't do that again.

Thanks for the little map. It let me see how far you had to travel in your canoe. I'm glad you didn't have to paddle all the time.

I didn't know Ho Chi Minh City was so big. Coming from a village, I feel confused in the city, too. You seem to be having fun just the same, seeing all the new sights.

An outdoor city market where vendors sell food and other items.

I wish I could go to the market with you. I could almost taste the appetizing meat broth you had there. I think I might like it—rice and all! Mom makes a meat broth with tomatoes and other things in it. It's so good on a cold night!

The fish fry at the market must have been fun. I've never been to a fish fry. There must have been quite a commotion with all the people waiting to get some!

Write soon. I want to know more about your trip to Ho Chi Minh City.

Michelle

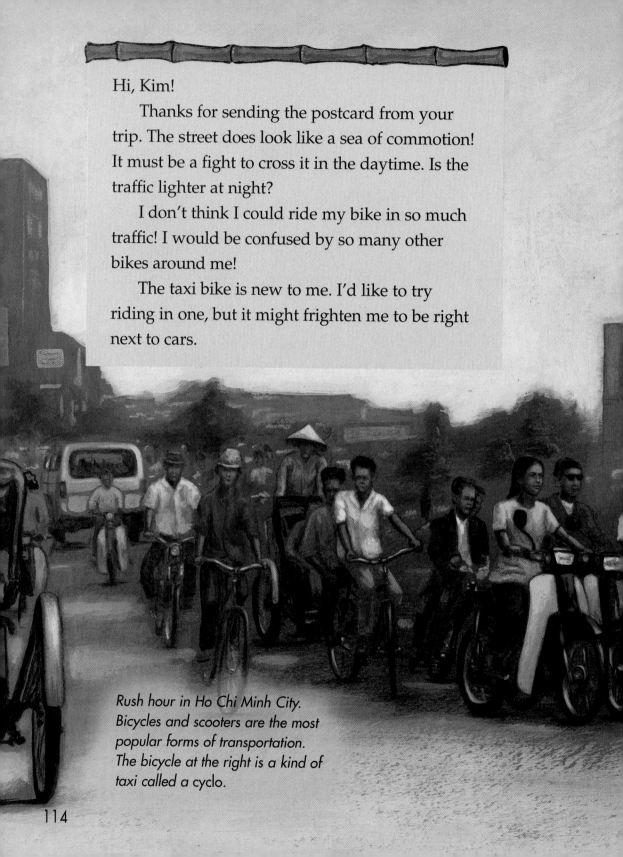

Hi, Kim!

Thanks for sending the postcard from your trip. The street does look like a sea of commotion! It must be a fight to cross it in the daytime. Is the traffic lighter at night?

I don't think I could ride my bike in so much traffic! I would be confused by so many other bikes around me!

The taxi bike is new to me. I'd like to try riding in one, but it might frighten me to be right next to cars.

Rush hour in Ho Chi Minh City. Bicycles and scooters are the most popular forms of transportation. The bicycle at the right is a kind of taxi called a cyclo.

I see that people in Vietnam dress much the way people here do. I was surprised to hear that girls don't go out in shorts. Everyone here lives in them when it's hot!

It was kind of you to invite us to visit. My mom is thinking about it. Our neighbor, Mrs. Tran, might be traveling this year to visit her mother in Vietnam. We might be able to travel together! It would be good to have our interpreter with us.

Write soon,
Michelle

Kim!

I am hysterically happy! Tonight my mom said
we can visit you in August for a week. All right!

We need to make plans. The plane flies to Ho Chi
Minh City. Mrs. Tran's brother will meet our flight,
and then take us to meet you at the market. Will we
travel in your canoe?

Isn't all of this amazing? First we write to each
other. Then you invite me to visit. Before long we'll
meet!

Write soon, and I'll see you in August!

Michelle

Think About It

1. What are three things that Michelle and Kim have in common? What are three things that are different in their lives?

2. How do you think Kim feels about having Michelle come to visit?

3. Imagine that you are Michelle and that you have visited Kim. Write a thank-you letter to Kim and her family.

Wolf Pack
SOUNDS AND SIGNALS

by Kana Riley

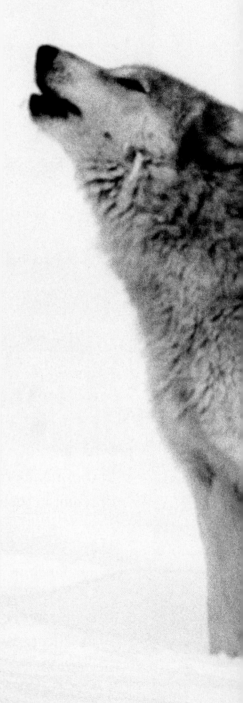

A wolf howls across the tundra. Then comes another howl and another across the arctic land. Each wolf makes its own sound. Together, the pack is like a musical group, with each singer sounding a different note.

Wolves live in family groups called packs. Howling is one of the ways the pack members talk to each other.

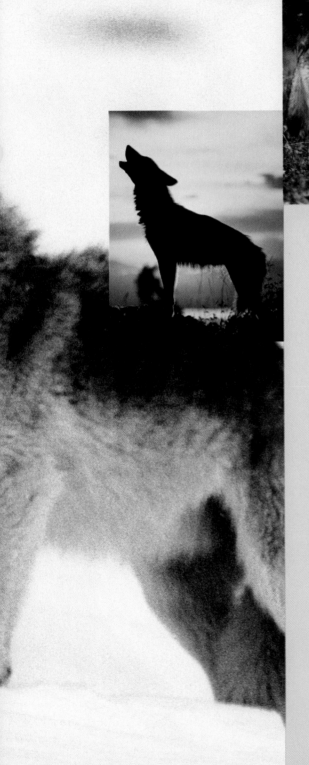

Wolves have a lot to say. Sometimes they howl loudly to call the pack together. At other times the howls say "keep out" to outsiders, wolves that are not part of the family.

Important times call for howls. If a pack member is injured, it howls for help. If the injured wolf dies, all the other wolves howl piteously. When pups are born, pack members howl their pleasure.

In wolf society, howls are not the only way to talk. An angry wolf growls. The other wolves understand this message and know to stay away.

If a wolf is feeling friendly, it may squeak like a mouse. Wolves squeak when they are bonding with each other. A mother wolf squeaks when she talks to her pups.

Like the dogs they are related to, wolves also bark. That sound signals excitement, perhaps at a new scent.

Each wolf pack has two leaders, the alpha male and the alpha female. The alpha animals have ways to signal the others that they are boss.

Sometimes they use their tails. A tail held up shows that the alpha wolf is proud to be the leader. When another wolf meets an alpha wolf, it holds its tail down, showing that it is willing to surrender its power to the leader.

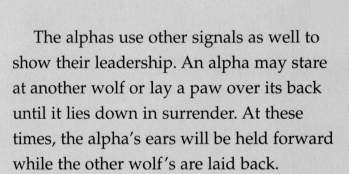

The alphas use other signals as well to show their leadership. An alpha may stare at another wolf or lay a paw over its back until it lies down in surrender. At these times, the alpha's ears will be held forward while the other wolf's are laid back.

To be strong leaders, the alpha wolves must have the cooperation of the pack. Most of the time, using these gentle ways, they can get it without a struggle.

Wolves have abundant ways to display their cooperation. Are pack members licking an alpha wolf's muzzle? Is a wolf holding another's snout in its mouth? Is a wolf wagging its tail? All of these are messages, too. They are ways members of the pack tell one another they are friends.

123

When pups become part of the pack, they must practice the skills they will need in the future. They learn wolf talk, an important skill. They leap around with tails wagging. Then their noses pick up a scent, and they begin to howl with excitement. "Look at us!" they seem to say. "We're learning how to be members of the society of wolves."

Their little howls mix with those of the grown-up pack members. The sound sends a clear message. The song of the wolf will not cease to be heard across the tundra.

Think About It

1. How do wolves communicate with each other? Give an example and explain its meaning.

2. Why do you think it is important for a wolf pack to have strong leaders?

3. If you heard a pack of wolves howling in the wild, what would you think? Write about how you would feel and why.

Who Invented This?

by Beverly A. Dietz • illustrated by Debbie Tilley

Let me have a bit of that. I need to correct another mistake.

Pencils were used long before there were erasers. To correct mistakes, people tried many kinds of things to remove their pencil marks.

Rubber erasers were first used in the 1700s. Still, finding an eraser when you needed one could be a problem.

Then, in 1858, two inventors had the same bright idea. Both Hyman Lipman and Joseph Rechendorfer invented pencils with erasers right on the end of them.

I'm going to get a patent for this!

I'm going to get a patent for this!

For a long time, shoppers took their own baskets to market to put their food into. Since the baskets didn't have much space, people couldn't get much in one trip.

Sylvan Goldman owned an early supermarket. He wanted shoppers at his store to get a lot of food—more than they could put into their baskets. In 1937, Goldman had an idea. What if shoppers had carts on wheels, carts that could hold lots of food? He invented the shopping cart.

Before 1904, many people ate ice cream—but only out of dishes. At the World's Fair held that summer, the people selling ice cream ran out of dishes.

Ernest Hamwi was selling thin waffles at the fair. He rolled some waffles into cones. People could put their ice cream into the circular opening of the cone. Just like that, he invented ice-cream cones!

John Spilsbury invented picture puzzles more than 200 years ago. He wanted to help teach children about places around the world. He began by painting maps on wood. Then he cut the maps apart so that children could put them together again.

Spilsbury's maps were the very first picture puzzles. Now kids and grown-ups alike put puzzles together just for fun.

Walter Hunt was an inventor. In 1825, he needed some money. A man handed him a piece of wire. He said he would pay Hunt $400 for any invention he could make from it.

Hunt's response was almost automatic. He knew well the problems people had with pins. Hunt invented the safety pin and got his $400. However, the other man then owned Hunt's idea, and it made him rich.

You can see that not all inventions are complicated and expensive. Some of the little things we use every day are important inventions.

Do you have an idea for an invention of your own? You may want to modify something people already use. Maybe you'll invent a brand-new device. Then one day someone might use your invention and ask, "Who invented this?"

Think About It

1. What have you learned about the reasons people have for inventing things?

2. How do you think Walter Hunt felt about inventing the safety pin?

3. You've invented something new, and it's a success! Write a news story about your invention that the local newspaper could print.

Just Curious

If you're curious about an invention, you're eager to learn more about it. Centuries ago, this wouldn't have been the case. Back then *curious*, which comes from the Latin word for *care*, meant being careful about something. Here are some things you might be curious about.

Why do people drive on a parkway and
    park on a driveway?

Why is it that if you wrap something you
    put the wrapping on, but if you peel
    something, you take the peel off?

Is yesterday's newspaper an
    oldspaper?

Why aren't there any nuts in
    doughnuts?

Do fish ever get thirsty?

133

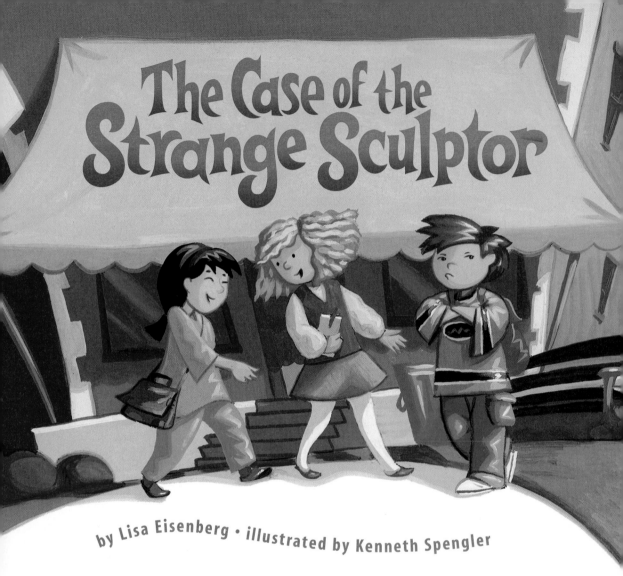

The Case of the Strange Sculptor

by Lisa Eisenberg · illustrated by Kenneth Spengler

It was an important day in the village of Fudge Corners. All the citizens had come to the village square to see the work of a local sculptor revealed. Gina Ginetti, well-known girl detective, was there with her friends Angela and Al.

"I'm so excited!" Angela exclaimed. "Today's the day we get to see Reggie Rodgers's statue of the Gentle Giant. It's supposed to be his finest work yet!"

"I don't see what all the fuss is about," Al muttered.

"The Gentle Giant is Fudge Corners's best-known dog!"
Angela retorted. "He saved the life of the village's founder,
Felix Fudge, in 1809."

"The Gentle Giant is fine," said Al. "It's Reggie Rodgers
I don't like. He got first prize in the art show last year, and
he's bragged about it ever since!"

Angela frowned. "Maybe the reason you don't like
Reggie is that he's a better sculptor than you are!"

"*I'm* the better sculptor," Al insisted. "*He's* just the
better boaster."

"Oh, stop arguing, you two," Gina broke in. "Look! They're about to unveil the statue!"

The mayor of Fudge Corners retold the story of how the Gentle Giant had saved Felix Fudge. He also spoke about how lucky their village was to have a fine sculptor like Reggie Rodgers. Then he swept away the sheet that had hidden the statue.

"Ohhhh," cried the crowd. "The dog looks so lifelike! What a genius Rodgers is!" A flock of pigeons fluttered down to investigate.

Everyone clapped, except for Al. His mouth dropped open and he gaped at the platform. "That's *my* statue of the Gentle Giant! I made it in my basement, and it was still there last night. Someone stole it, and I know who's guilty. Reggie Rodgers, that's who!"

Angela put her arm around her excited friend. "Come on now, Al. We know you don't like Reggie Rodgers, but that's no reason to make up wild stories!"

"I *did* make it! I wanted to see if I could do a better job than Reggie. I was certain I could," declared Al.

Angela glanced nervously around the crowded square. "Everyone is looking at us strangely. You'd better pipe down, Al."

"Wait a second, Angela," Gina put in. "I can't remember Al ever telling a lie. I believe him!"

"What reason could Reggie have for taking Al's statue?" Angela asked. "It doesn't seem logical."

"I don't know, but I trust my detective's instinct," Gina said. "Let's find him and talk to him straightaway!"

Al found the support of Gina and Angela strengthening as they searched the large crowd. When they located Reggie Rodgers, Al marched right up to him. "Why did you steal my statue?" he asked.

Reggie sneered. "Ha! Why would I sneak into your basement and steal your sad little statue?"

"I don't know!" Al yelled. "Maybe yours didn't come out right, or maybe you didn't finish on time."

Reggie glanced around nervously. "That's crazy! I don't even know where you live, and besides, I have an alibi for last night."

"I've done it again!" Gina bragged. "I've cracked another case. Reggie, whatever your alibi is for last night, it's a fake. *You* know you stole Al's statue, and *I* know you're guilty. You gave yourself away twice!"

How did Gina know that Reggie had stolen Al's statue?

Solution: Reggie said he didn't know where Al lived, but he knew the statue had been in the basement. Also, he knew the statue had been stolen last night!

Think About It

1. How is Gina able to solve the mystery?

2. How do you think Reggie feels when the mayor reveals the statue of the Gentle Giant? How do you think he feels when Gina, Al, and Angela come rushing up to him?

3. What do you think happens after Gina shows that Reggie is guilty? Write the next part of the story.

Just Enough Is Plenty

by Sydnie Meltzer Kleinhenz • illustrated by Normand Cousineau

A farmer earned just enough to live a simple life. Being of a thrifty character, he insisted on saving every extra coin. Over time, his savings grew to a generous sum. He became fascinated with his riches—and highly annoying to his friends and neighbors.

"I'm rich now, but don't worry," he said to a friend. "I'll still talk to you."

Being of a rascally character, his friend saw a chance for fun. "How can I know you're rich," he said, "unless I see some evidence?"

The friend had made a roguish plan with neighbors to stop the farmer from boasting. Now he said, "I seldom boast, but I'm rich, too. I own all the fields on this road."

"Really?" the farmer asked.

"It's the truth," insisted the friend. "Just ask your neighbors."

"Hmm," said the farmer. He set off down the road to investigate. As he passed rows of corn, beans, and melons, he asked his neighbors, "Whose fields are these?"

143

The neighbors stuck to the plan. They told him the fields belonged to his friend.

The farmer promptly purchased extra land. Meanwhile, the friend borrowed neighbors' pigs and hens. Then he visited the farmer, who was toiling in his new fields. His clothes were soiled and his face was wet.

"Hello," called the friend.

"Hello, friend!" the farmer called back. He pointed to his fields. "Now you see I'm a rich man."

"You will harvest more than enough for a rich man!" his friend said. "I seldom boast, but I'm very rich myself. I've just purchased ten more pigs and twenty more hens."

That night, the farmer crept to his friend's yard to see if he really had more animals. "It's the truth!" he whispered.

The next day, he purchased more pigs and hens. There was a lot of extra oinking and clucking.

The farmer spent the day waving hens away from windows, guarding his crops from pigs, and toiling in the sun.

When his friend arrived, the farmer pointed to the animals and said, "Now you see I'm a rich man." Then off he dashed to guard his corn from hungry pigs. He crept back so tired that he plopped in a chair, smashing an egg a hen had laid there.

"You'll have more than enough ham and eggs for a rich man," his friend said. "Yet this hut of yours does not look like the home of a rich man. No one passing by would guess that you're rich. You need a fine, big house now."

The farmer was annoyed. "What!" he said. "How would I find time to work on a big, new house? I don't have time now even to think." He stomped off.

That night, the farmer did think. He looked around his cozy hut. It was just right for him. He didn't want a big house—or all those fields and animals that made him so tired. He knew what he needed to do.

The next day, the farmer joyfully gave away his fields, pigs, and hens. He was left with just enough, and that was plenty.

Think About It

1. Why does the thrifty farmer purchase more fields and more animals? Why does he give them away?

2. How do you think the thrifty farmer feels after he gives his fields and animals away?

3. What do you think the farmer's neighbors say when he gives away what he has purchased? Write their conversation.

Barnyard Baloney

What happened to the duck that flew upside down?

    It quacked up.

What kind of stories do little pigs enjoy most?

    Pig tales.

What did the doctor put on the pig's sore foot?

    Antibiotic oinkment.

How can you keep a pet goat from smelling?

    By stopping up its nose.

Why is a goose like an icicle?

    They both grow down.

What did the pony say when it had a sore throat?

    "Sorry, I'm just a little horse."

Big Bad Wolf and the Law

by Deborah Eaton   illustrated by Terry Hoff

Big Bad Wolf

TIME:

August, some year

PLACE:

Storyland Court

Judge Bo Peep

Lawyer

Bailiff

Red Riding Cap

BAILIFF: Order in the court! All rise for Judge Peep.

JUDGE PEEP: Be seated. Let's launch right into this. What is the charge?

LAWYER *(hands judge a paper)***:** Attempted eating, Judge.

JUDGE *(discards paper)***:** Well, that's original. Usually eating is acceptable, isn't it?

LAWYER: Yes, but Mr. Wolf was found chasing a grandma and her little granddaughter.

JUDGE: That's awful!

WOLF *(worried)***:** I didn't do it!

JUDGE: Well, let's get on with it. I've been up since dawn *(yawns)*, and I've got lost sheep that have to be caught.

BAILIFF: Mr. Big B. Wolf! Please stand and raise your right paw.

WOLF *(paw up)*: I'm honored to be here, Your Honor. Allow me to say that I never saw such a beautiful judge.

LAWYER: I object! Attempted flattery!

JUDGE: I'll allow it. *(looks in pocket mirror)* It shows he's truthful. Now, call your first witness.

BAILIFF: Little Red Riding Cap!

LAWYER: What caused you to accuse the wolf, Miss Cap?

RED CAP: He . . . he . . . *(begins to bawl)*

LAWYER: He what?

RED CAP: He said my grandma would be *delicious*! *(cries louder)*

LAWYER *(triumphantly)*: You see? He did it!

WOLF *(desperately)*: No! I didn't! I'm innocent!

JUDGE *(chin in hand)*: I'm so worried about my sheep.

WOLF: Sheep? Sheep are delicious, too. Usually I like them in mint sauce, but . . .

JUDGE: That's it. HE DID IT!

LAWYER: And he isn't even repentant!

BAILIFF: Haul him off to jail!

WOLF: Wait! This is such an injustice! It's the author's fault, not mine! I was just following the original script! My name is really Big *Bill* Wolf! I'm a real sweet pea!

LAWYER: Ha! Ha! Tell us another one!

WOLF: It's the truth! I'm a victim of circumstances. We all are! Just look at you, Judge! You *can't* like that ruffled dress and awkward bonnet. You have them on because they're drawn on you in every story.

JUDGE: Well, I . . .

WOLF: And you! *(points a claw at Red Riding Cap)* Do you really want to go to your grandma's all the time? Wouldn't you rather go bowling or something?

RED CAP: Bowling?

WOLF: Aw, I'd never eat the kid, Judge. I'd never put a paw on her.

JUDGE: So you didn't eat my sheep?

WOLF: Why, I wouldn't hurt a flea. *(scratches)* I'm not big and bad, just ask my mother. Ask anyone!

LAWYER: Let's ask my surprise witnesses. *(nods to bailiff)*

JUDGE: Who are they?

BAILIFF: The three little pigs!

WOLF *(sinking into chair)***:** Uh-oh.

Think About It

1. Why is the wolf charged with attempted eating? How does he try to defend himself?

2. Why does the wolf sink into his chair and say "Uh-oh" at the end of the play?

3. What do you think the judge will decide at the end of the case? What will the wolf say and do? Write another scene for the play.

A Clever Plan

by María Santos

illustrated by
Sylvie Daigneault

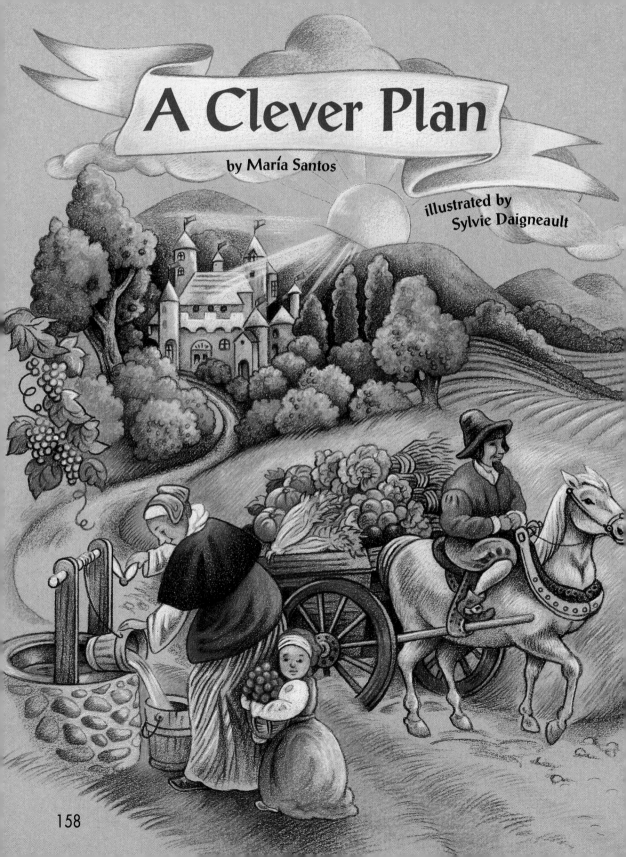

The kingdom of Woodlandia was a good place to live, most of the time. For many years, fine harvests had supplied the people with plenty to eat. Their land was free from famine. Their kingdom was named for its thick woodlands, so the Woodlandians were also plentifully supplied with firewood. The only problem they had from time to time was their king.

King Roger was kind, as a good leader should be. He believed that kindness was very important. He always rewarded his subjects when they were kind to their fellow Woodlandians.

You might ask, "If the king was so kind, what was the problem?" Well, King Roger had a lot of ideas for rewarding his subjects, but his ideas weren't always clever.

One time a kind shoemaker made a pair of wooden shoes for the king. No shoes had ever fit him as perfectly as these did. "If only my subjects were as lucky as I am," he said, sighing. "They would never again have to put up with uncomfortable shoes." Then a not-so-clever idea came to him.

King Roger proclaimed a royal decree. Everyone in every province of the kingdom was to have shoes exactly like his. For, as King Roger knew, the size and shape were perfect.

The same thing happened when King Roger returned with a pet tiger from a royal journey he took. No pet had ever pleased him as this one did. He decreed that everyone in Woodlandia was to keep a pet tiger. For, as King Roger knew, this kind of pet was perfect.

For a long time the Woodlandians lived with King Roger's decrees because he was such a kind leader. They did not want to hurt his feelings, as he would never hurt theirs.

Things changed when the latest royal decree was proclaimed. This is how it happened. King Roger looked at his newest robe, the one with the satin hood. It was trimmed with a thousand gleaming pearls and a thousand glittering emeralds. It sparkled like a billion stars!

Oh, he looked splendid! Who wouldn't feel happy dressed in outfits like his? To bring this joy to his subjects, he decreed that everyone was to dress as he did.

The Woodlandians stood still. They looked at each other. How could they dress like the king? They did not have silks and satins. They did not have billions of pearls and emeralds.

The mayor of Woodlandia understood the problem. He called together the ministers from every province in the kingdom. They looked through rare old books of wisdom, hoping to find a solution.

After many hours, the oldest minister said, "I have an idea."

"Please, tell us what it is!" they implored. When they heard it, all agreed it was a clever plan.

On the day the new dress code took effect, the Woodlandians went to the palace. They wanted to show King Roger their fine robes. The king just stood there, looking confused. Before long, however, he understood what his subjects had done. He shook with laughter until tears trickled down his cheeks.

King Roger took a walk among the people. He looked at each costume with delight. "These emeralds are . . . ?" he asked.

"Grapes, your majesty," the grocer's wife replied.

"Those plumes . . . ?"

"Twigs, your majesty," said the woodcutter.

163

"People of Woodlandia," announced the king, "I wish to make a royal decree."

"Oh, no!" whispered the mayor, as he shook in his wooden shoes. "Our clever plan didn't work!"

"I proclaim that from now on, before I make a royal decree, I will meet with the ministers of every province. Perhaps they will tell me when my clever ideas are not so clever!"

King Roger was glad that his loyal subjects had shown him his mistake in this kind way. He rewarded them with a royal picnic in the royal woods, and everyone had a royal time!

Think About It

1. What problem do the people of Woodlandia have with their king?

2. What lesson does the king learn about being kind to his subjects?

3. King Roger does not want anyone to miss his royal picnic. Create a poster he could use to announce the event.

Fire in the

by Caren B. Stelson   illustrated by Carmelo Blandino

Remember Smokey Bear, the forest ranger's best friend? Smokey always said it was everyone's job to take care of the forest. He said, "Only YOU can prevent forest fires." That's still true, but times have changed.

Forest rangers no longer believe that all fires are bad. In fact, rangers now think that some fires may even be good for a forest.

Forest

Since leaping flames destroy trees, you might ask, "How can a fire be good for a forest?" It seems that fire is the way a forest renews itself.

Fire burns old branches, underbrush, and diseased trees. The ashes from these make the soil richer, and more sunlight reaches the forest floor. This leads to fast growth of strong, new trees. Today, forest rangers think of fire as an important part of a forest's life cycle.

Deciding which fires to let burn and which to put out is a challenge for forest rangers. If people and homes are in danger, rangers are quick to call in help.

Firefighters and volunteers put on their gear—helmets with face masks and fireproof coats and gloves. They bring their equipment—shovels, axes, and hoes. Planes drop chemicals that make the forest less flammable, slowing the billowing flames. The planes may also dip huge buckets in a nearby lake and pour water on the fire.

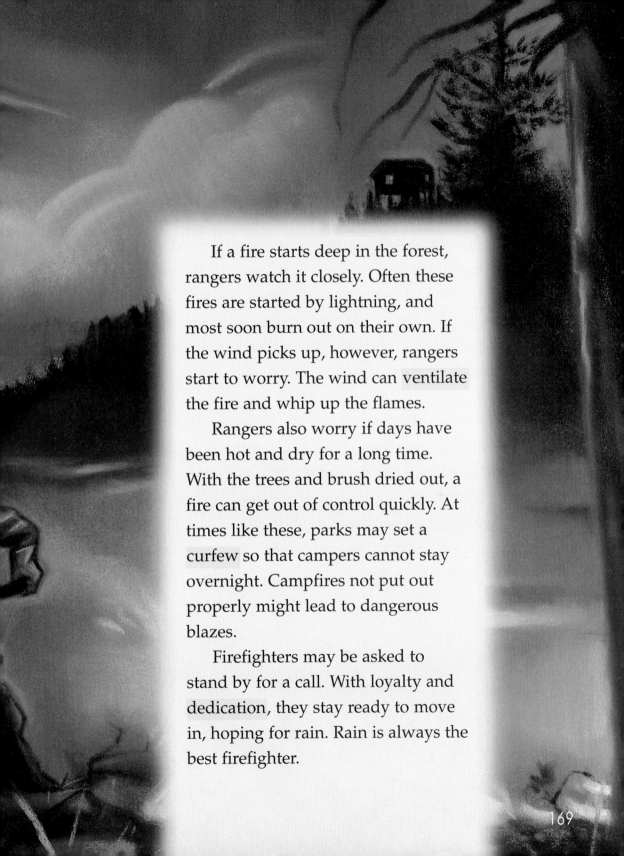

If a fire starts deep in the forest, rangers watch it closely. Often these fires are started by lightning, and most soon burn out on their own. If the wind picks up, however, rangers start to worry. The wind can ventilate the fire and whip up the flames.

Rangers also worry if days have been hot and dry for a long time. With the trees and brush dried out, a fire can get out of control quickly. At times like these, parks may set a curfew so that campers cannot stay overnight. Campfires not put out properly might lead to dangerous blazes.

Firefighters may be asked to stand by for a call. With loyalty and dedication, they stay ready to move in, hoping for rain. Rain is always the best firefighter.

In 1988, rangers faced a serious fire challenge in Yellowstone National Park. It was a hot summer, and the forest was extremely dry. There had been little snow that year, and it had hardly rained at all for six weeks.

When lightning started fires deep in the forest, rangers decided it was safe to let them burn. Then the wind picked up, and everything changed. Flames 200 feet tall leaped and roared. They started new fires and rekindled old ones.

The strong winds sent smoke billowing over the park. Visitors and cabins were now at risk. Firefighters from many cities arrived with their equipment. Brigades of volunteers put on firefighting gear, too. All joined forces, but each time they seemed to have the blaze under control, it rekindled.

The fires raged all summer. Finally, in September, it started to rain, and the fires at last sputtered out. Millions of trees had been lost, but the forest itself had not been destroyed. By the next summer, a new carpet of grass and millions of wildflowers covered the hillsides. The forest had started to heal. The cycle of life had begun once again.

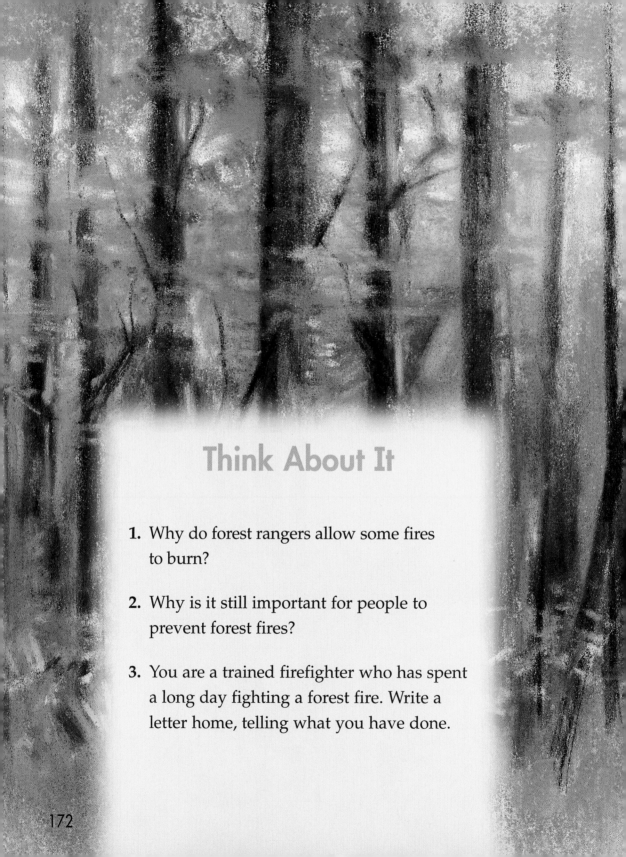

Think About It

1. Why do forest rangers allow some fires to burn?

2. Why is it still important for people to prevent forest fires?

3. You are a trained firefighter who has spent a long day fighting a forest fire. Write a letter home, telling what you have done.

Mix 'Em Up

When you rearrange the letters of a word to make another word, you've formed an *anagram*. For example, the letters of *Sue* can be rearranged to make *use; grape juice* can become *a jug recipe.*

Here are some others.

    astronomers = moon starers
    schoolmaster = the classroom
    snooze alarms = Alas! No more *z*'s.

Try these in math class.

    a decimal point = I'm a dot in place.
    eleven plus two = twelve plus one

Amaze your friends with these:

    Heavy rain? = Hire a navy!
    vacation times = I'm not as active.

This one may be your teacher's favorite.

    listen = silent

A Place of New Beginnings

by Ben Farrell   illustrated by Jui Ishida

"This is Ellis Island, Karen," Dad said, "where my father's grandfather began his new life. By coming to the United States, Poppa Joe enriched the lives of our entire family."

"Did he come to this place to qualify for citizenship?" I asked.

"No," Dad said. "He came to Ellis Island as a petitioner to enter the United States. Petitioners were obliged to see an examiner here before going to the mainland."

"Why?" I asked.

"That's one of the things we'll learn about on the tour," Dad said.

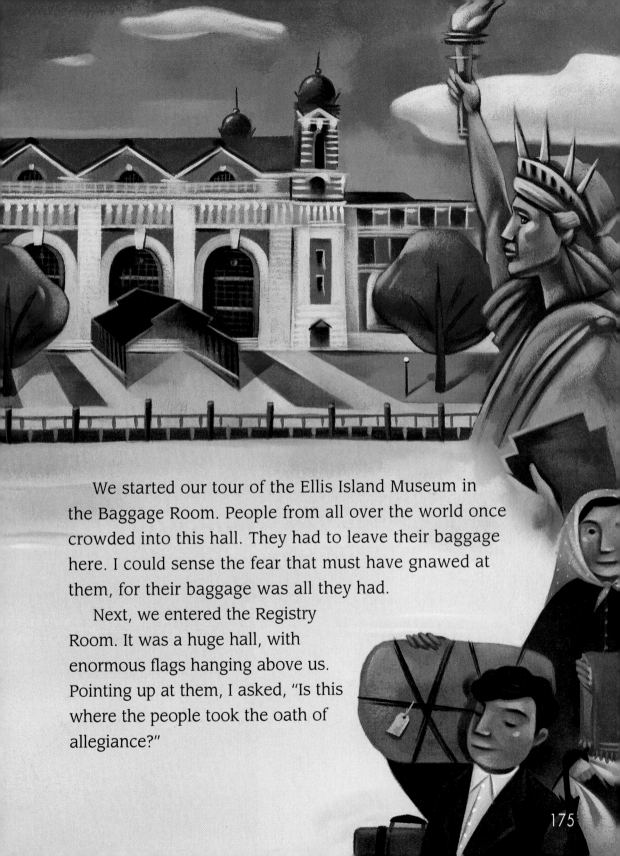

We started our tour of the Ellis Island Museum in the Baggage Room. People from all over the world once crowded into this hall. They had to leave their baggage here. I could sense the fear that must have gnawed at them, for their baggage was all they had.

Next, we entered the Registry Room. It was a huge hall, with enormous flags hanging above us. Pointing up at them, I asked, "Is this where the people took the oath of allegiance?"

"No," Dad said. "They didn't take the oath of allegiance until later, at the citizenship hearing. It takes time and study to become a citizen. This was just the starting place."

"I guess I have a lot to learn," I apologized. "What did happen in this room?"

"This is where the examiner checked passengers' documents," Dad said. "Ships had to provide certificates that gave facts about each passenger."

"What did the examiner check for?" I asked.

"They asked where the person had come from and what he or she intended to do in the United States. Doctors had to check the people, too."

"I guess they had to know if the people were healthy," I said.

"Yes," Dad replied, "but they were mainly checking for diseases. They didn't want to endanger the lives of people living in the United States. Immigrants with a disease were sent back to their homelands."

176

I looked around the hall. How it must have resounded with noise when it was filled with people! Many would be talking excitedly about getting into the United States. Some would be worrying about being sent back.

"Did Grandpop's grandmother come to Ellis Island, too?" I asked.

"I think so," Dad said, "but no one knows what her name was before she married. The tradition of women changing their names when they marry makes them hard to trace."

"That tradition must be changing," I said. "Some of my friends' moms have kept their names. I think I will, too."

Dad laughed and said, "It's a pity they didn't do things that way in those earlier days." I laughed, too, but I felt a little sad about our family history being lost.

Then Dad said, "Just the same, it might be possible to find out about her. We'd have to do some serious digging."

"Let's do it, Dad," I urged. "I'll help—I like doing research!"

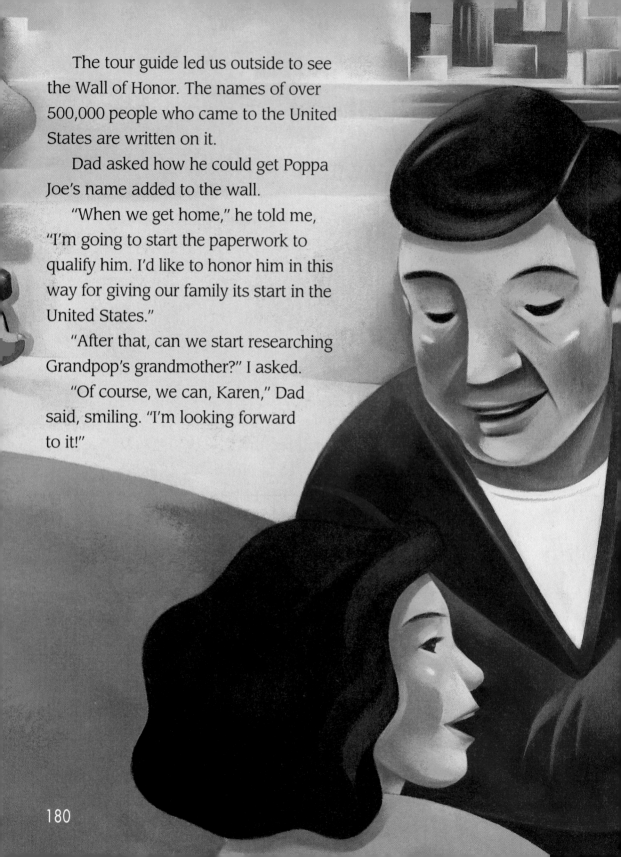

The tour guide led us outside to see the Wall of Honor. The names of over 500,000 people who came to the United States are written on it.

Dad asked how he could get Poppa Joe's name added to the wall.

"When we get home," he told me, "I'm going to start the paperwork to qualify him. I'd like to honor him in this way for giving our family its start in the United States."

"After that, can we start researching Grandpop's grandmother?" I asked.

"Of course, we can, Karen," Dad said, smiling. "I'm looking forward to it!"

Think About It

1. Why do Karen and her dad visit Ellis Island?

2. How do you think Poppa Joe felt when he arrived at Ellis Island?

3. Imagine that you visit Ellis Island and send a postcard to a friend. Write a message for that postcard.

Desert Animals

by David Delgado

illustrated by Michael Maydak

It's daytime in the desert. The sun shines brightly in the clear sky, and the air is hot and dry. The sand and rocks are hot and rough.

The desert looks empty, with only tall, spiny cactuses to be seen. One tough old cactus has died of disease and toppled over. Now it decomposes as it lies on the burning desert floor.

Scrubby bushes grow in the desert, too. The low branches of this brush offer desert creatures a little shade from the burning sun.

At first glance, the desert doesn't seem to be the habitat of many creatures. If you take a closer look, however, you'll see that it is crowded with animals! These creatures have adapted to the harsh climate and geography of the desert. They can live where other animals could not survive.

If you stir up the sand, you will find that it is teeming with life. Many insects, such as ants, beetles, and even bees, dig burrows. Staying underground protects the bugs from the blazing sun.

The digger bee makes a long, narrow tunnel beneath the sand. Here it stores pollen for food and lays a single egg. The baby bee will spend the first phase of its life growing underground.

In the shade under the brush, a lizard is trying to keep cool. Lizards will perch on a branch to get away from the heat of the ground. You might laugh to see the zebra-tailed lizard running on its back feet. It does this to keep its front feet and body up off the hot sand.

Plodding along nearby is a big, slow-moving reptile that looks like a land-dwelling turtle. Its tough shell protects it from the sun's hot rays. It gets enough water from the plants it eats. One of its favorite foods is cactus flowers.

A rattlesnake is asleep in the shade of a rock. Rattlers rest during the heat of the day and come out to hunt and eat at night.

The jackrabbit has big ears that help keep it from getting too hot. They provide more skin to let off extra body heat.

Birds live in the desert, too. The small ones that hover in the air are hummingbirds. They sip nectar from cactus flowers.

The roadrunner spends most of its time on the ground. It dines on insects and small animals.

The big, dark birds high in the sky are buzzards. They are looking for the bodies of animals dead from disease. In eating them, they keep the desert clean.

A night photograph would show the desert to be crowded, not empty. Bats fly out to dine on the buzzing insects. Coyotes prowl far and wide, hunting snakes, lizards, birds, and smaller mammals. The lonely howl of the coyote is the night song of the desert.

Day and night, the desert is alive with animals.

Think About It

1. What is the main problem for animals in the desert?

2. Why is it sometimes hard to see animals in the desert?

3. Choose one desert animal. What else would you like to know about that animal? Write four questions you want to have answered.

Step on No Pets

Take a look at the title of this page. After you've read it from left to right, read the letters from right to left. You've just discovered a *palindrome*. You'll find more of them below.

Don't nod.
Dee saw a seed.
Del saw a sled.
Did I draw Della too tall, Edward? I did!
A tin mug for a jar of gum, Nita.
Mr. Owl ate my metal worm.
A man, a plan, a canal. Panama.
Was it a bar or a bat I saw?

In another type of palindrome, it's the words, rather than the letters, in a sentence that read the same in both directions.

You can cage a swallow, can't you, but you can't swallow a cage, can you?

Foxes love chickens; few chickens love foxes.

189

School Days

by Susan McCloskey • illustrated by Thomas Buchs

Heather woke with a feeling of dread. Her family had just moved to a new community, and today would be her first day at her new school.

Heather had held her teacher at her old school in high regard and she missed her already. "I just know I'm going to loathe school here," she told herself with certainty.

She raised her head from her pillow and gazed outside. It was dark in the mornings now, and the cars still had their headlights on. The weather was cold, too. Heather snuggled down under the feathery warmth of her comforter.

190

Soon her mom rapped on her door. "Rise and shine, sleepyhead!" she called out heartily.

"Oh, Mom!" Heather said sulkily. "You don't have to be so cheery!"

Heather got dressed, pulling her red sweater over her head. Her cat was getting ready for the day, too, and she stopped to watch in amusement. He had finished washing himself, but a little tip of pink still protruded from his mouth. That always made Heather chuckle.

"Maybe I should lie and say I have a bad headache," Heather said to herself. "Mom and Dad would probably let me stay home." Then she remembered what her mom always told people. "Completely trustworthy—that's my Heather!" Faking a headache would not be being trustworthy. She was determined to deserve her mom's high regard.

Heather took a deep breath. Undoubtedly she would get through the day, but she was not looking forward to it.

It was her dad's custom to fix Heather a good breakfast on school days. Normally, they both enjoyed this custom. This morning, however, Heather felt indifferent to food.

"A good thing, too," she said, entering the kitchen. "There's no one here!"

She looked out the window and saw her parents laughing with a woman who was walking a dog. The woman looked pleasant and friendly. Heather wished she could join in the laughter, too.

193

Then the woman and her dog moved on, and her parents came back into the house.

"Ready for breakfast?" her dad asked. "What'll it be? French toast? Scrambled eggs? A dry crust of bread?" He was determined to cheer Heather up.

Heather couldn't help responding with amusement. "Just a healthy helping of whipped cream, please. Oh, and a little pie to go with it."

"I can see the headlines now," her dad went on. "Witty Girl Makes Hundreds of Friends in One Day!"

"I wish!" said Heather. "I'd like oatmeal for breakfast, please."

Feeling more cheerful, Heather ate heartily. "Who was that woman you were talking with?" she asked.

"You'll meet her soon enough," Mom said with a smile, picking a loose thread from Heather's skirt.

Just then there was a brisk knock on the door.

Heather opened it. There was the pleasant-looking woman.

"Hi, Heather," she said. "I'm your neighbor, Mrs. Weatherbee. Are you starting school today?"

"Yes, and I'm nervous about it," said Heather. "I'll miss my teacher at my old school. No one could be as nice as she was."

The woman's eyes twinkled as she laughed. "Well, Heather," she said, "I'm your *new* teacher, and I promise to try!"

Heather laughed, too. Maybe school wouldn't be so bad after all.

Think About It

1. Why does Heather dread the first day of school?

2. Heather sees her parents outside, talking and laughing with a woman who looks pleasant and friendly. What do you think they are talking about?

3. When Heather comes home from her first day at her new school, she writes in her diary. Write Heather's diary entry telling about the day's events and her feelings about them.

WHEN I WAS EIGHT

by Roberto Aguas, Jr.
(as told to Diane Hoyt-Goldsmith)

My name is Roberto Aguas (roh•BAIR•toh
AH•gwahs), Jr. I have the same first name as my
father and my grandfather, so everyone calls me
Junior.

My sister and I were born in California and have
lived here all our lives. Our parents, however, were
born in Mexico. That's why our family speaks
Spanish at home and why our Mexican culture is
so important to us.

Our grandparents live in Mexico, but we have many other relatives who live in California. Aunts, uncles, and cousins often come to visit us.

When I was eight years old, my grandparents came to stay with us for a month. They traveled from a small town in Jalisco (hah•LEES•koh), Mexico, where they know all their neighbors. I have good memories of that visit because I learned to do something that was interesting and fun!

Tortillas (tawr•TEE•yuhz) have always been one of my favorite foods. On that visit, my grandmother taught my sister and me how to make them. For the first time in my life, I helped make the tortillas for a family celebration.

My grandmother used a kind of flour called *masa* (MAH•sah), made from ground corn. She measured it carefully. Then she mixed it with water, salt, baking powder, and lard. She stirred all this into a big, sticky mass.

My grandmother showed my sister and me how to break off little balls and flatten them with our fingers. Then they looked like little pancakes!

The rolling out came next. My grandmother put some masa on the surface of the table to prevent sticking. When she rolled out a little pancake, it got bigger as it got flatter. We practiced rolling tortillas on the floury surface until ours were as flat and round as hers. We pretended we were cooks in a Mexican restaurant!

We had a family celebration with the tortillas my sister and I made. We ate them with chile, beans, and a *salsa* (SAHL•sah) made from tomatoes. They tasted delicious! Everyone complimented us on our cooking.

My mother always puts an extra chile pepper on the table for my father. No matter how much chile she puts into a dish she is cooking, he always wants it hotter! My father says that my mother's cooking is better than any you could get in a Mexican restaurant.

While we ate, my parents told us about the celebrations they had when they were children in Mexico. They like to share their memories of the *fiestas* (fee•ES•tahz) in the little towns where they grew up.

Children went to the town square with their cousins and all their relatives. People brought accordions and guitars along, and soon there was music for dancing. The smell of burning mesquite filled the night air as people put steaks on the grill to barbecue.

People ate, danced, and talked to their neighbors. They all had a great time. The next day, the town square was empty. Only the colorful confetti on the ground showed that a celebration had taken place.

Most of the time we still get our tortillas at the store. Just the same, my sister and I are glad that we learned how to make them at home. Now that our grandparents are far away in Mexico again, we have good memories of that happy day.

Think About It

1. Why does Junior have good memories of his grandparents' visit?

2. How does Junior feel about his Mexican culture? How can you tell?

3. Think about a celebration you have been to, such as a picnic or a party. List the sights, sounds, and smells of the celebration. Write a paragraph to describe what it was like to be there.

THE WEST BECKONS

by Ben Farrell • illustrated by Jerry Dadds

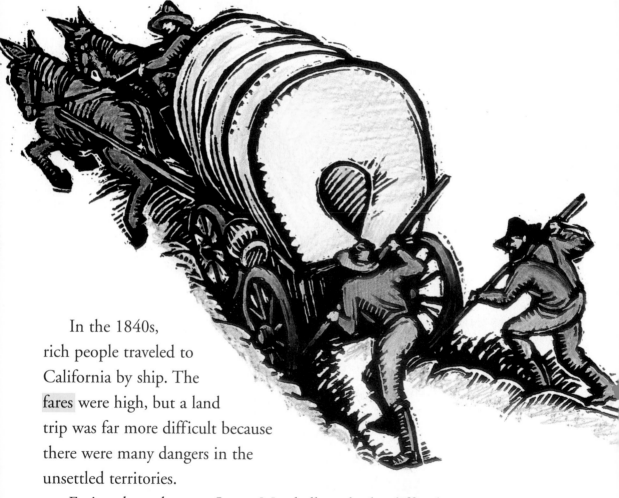

In the 1840s, rich people traveled to California by ship. The fares were high, but a land trip was far more difficult because there were many dangers in the unsettled territories.

Facing those dangers, James Marshall made the difficult trip west by wagon train. He hoped to make his fortune in California. He knew there would be few comforts there, but he was rugged and used to hard work.

Some time later, Marshall found
work with John Sutter. Soon the men
became partners in starting a sawmill
business, cutting logs into boards.
Sutter would provide the money, and
Marshall would build the mill. The
plan seemed workable.

Marshall was firmly convinced that
the sawmill would make his fortune.
A few months later, however, he made
a discovery that changed his life.

207

One morning, Marshall spotted a shiny stone in a ditch by the mill. Breathless, he lifted it out of the water. Then he saw another stone and quickly picked it up. The stones looked like gold!

Excitedly, Marshall showed the beautiful stones to his business partner. Sutter was sure they were gold, but he wasn't comfortable about the discovery. He really needed Marshall to keep working on the mill, as it was going to be far more profitable than a few small gold stones.

The discovery of gold was difficult to keep secret, and the word soon leaked out. Hopeful people came from all over with only one thing in mind—getting rich!

The gold seekers were a problem to Marshall because they were holding up work on the mill. To get rid of them, he sent them off to different parts of the unsettled territories. He didn't expect them to find anything.

However, the stream of people was endless. Sailors abandoned their ships and made their way inland. The gold rush was on!

By the time the mill was finished, Marshall had changed his mind about where his fortune lay. Now he was sure there was gold to be found. He promptly set out to find a claim of his own.

Marshall soon found out what had happened to the gold seekers he had heartlessly sent off. Many of them had found bountiful claims! Now they had the gold that might have been his.

The gold rush changed the lives of all those who had come from around the world. Only a few managed to become rich, but they all helped settle the land. They made California a multicultural state that today beckons travelers from around the world.

James Marshall never got rich from the gold rush his discovery started. He was still looking for gold when he died. Yet his name will never be forgotten. His find led to an important event in American history.

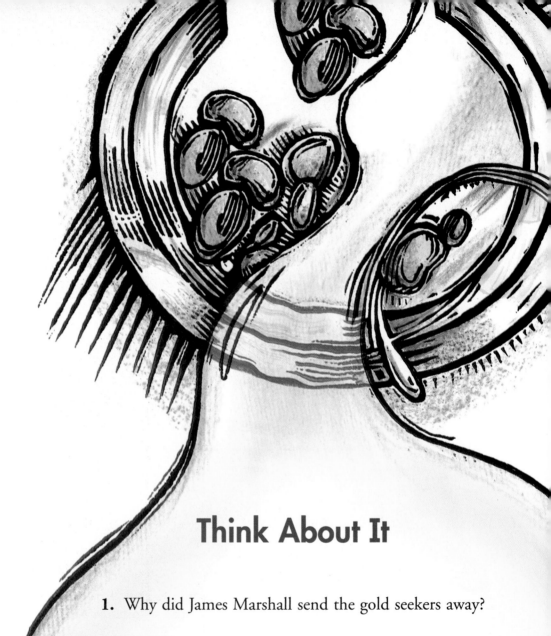

Think About It

1. Why did James Marshall send the gold seekers away?

2. Do you think Marshall's discovery helped or harmed California? Give reasons for your answer.

3. You are the owner of a store in California during Marshall's time. Make a poster offering items for sale that you think miners need. Use words and pictures on your poster.

A Song for Gold Miners

Here's a song the Gold Rush miners used to sing. Even though the words may be new to you, you probably know the tune: *"Oh, Susannah."*

I came from Salem City with my washpan on my knee.
I'm going to California now, the gold dust for to see.
It rained all night the day I left. The weather it was dry.
The sun so hot I froze to death. Susannah, don't you cry!
Oh, Susannah, oh, don't you cry for me!
I'm going to California now, my washpan on my knee!

I soon shall be in 'Frisco town, and there I'll look around,
And when I find some gold lumps there, I'll pick them off
   the ground.
I'll scrape the mountains clean, my dear, I'll drain the
   rivers dry,
A pocketful of rocks bring home, Susannah, don't you cry!
Oh, Susannah, oh, don't you cry for me!
I'm going to California now, my washpan on my knee!

Purple Mountain Majesty

by Deborah Akers • illustrated by Lane Dupont

Many of the first Americans traveled constantly.
Hunting for food ruled their lives, whether they lived
in the forest, desert, mountains, or plains.

At the foot of a great mountain, there was a place
where many tribes stopped to rest. It offered cool
springs for drinking and hot springs for soaking. Those
who visited left arrows or stones at the pools as they
wished for luck in the hunt. They believed that
the mountain kept their world in harmony.

Hundreds of years later, in 1806, a man named Zebulon Pike was exploring America's fertile plains and valleys. One day he saw the mountain from far away. It seemed to fill his imagination, and soon he was determined to climb it.

On a summer day, he and his crew set out, believing they could accomplish the climb by nightfall. They found that it took them two tough days just to get partway up! When it started to snow, they turned back. Pike wrote in his journal *No one will ever get up this mountain. It is an awful place!*

Even though he never got to the top, Zebulon Pike was remembered for his discovery. Pike himself had named the mountain Grand Peak, but mapmakers named it Pikes Peak in his honor. In 1820, a man named Stephen Long did make it to the top. When he looked around, he saw a place of endless possibilities.

In 1858, gold was discovered at Pikes Peak. Soon people were reading about this on city corners and in shady country arbors. One thought ran through many heads. *That place could give me everything I've always dreamed about.*

Thousands of people bought mining equipment and made the long, difficult journey across the wild, unsettled land. Soon the mountains were decorated with miners' huts, and makeshift towns sprang up overnight. For a while, the mountain did seem like a place where dreams could come true. People hoisted picks, dynamited hillsides, and searched through streambeds in the hope of finding gold. Life in the mines was very tough. A very few people got rich, but most of the rest lost everything.

When the gold ran out, the miners moved on. Although the mountain was left with holes and gashes, it was still a shining, beautiful place.

In later years, others went to the mountain in search of health. At the time, a disease called tuberculosis, or TB, harmed many people's lungs. Some said the clean, pure mountain air could help heal the lungs of TB sufferers.

Some people got better, and some did not, but all agreed that the mountain was an amazing place. Many people stayed and built a town. Pioneers heading out West often decided to settle near Pikes Peak. For many pioneers, Pikes Peak was their first glimpse of the great Rocky Mountains.

As the town grew, the mountain changed. A cog railroad hoisted visitors to the top, and soon there was a road, too. One thing stayed the same, though. The mountain remained a place of hopes and dreams.

In 1893, a woman named Katharine Lee Bates went to the top of Pikes Peak. She accomplished something wonderful up there. As she looked out at the miles of open sky, her imagination took flight. She wrote in her journal *Oh beautiful for spacious skies . . .* Her words became the song so many would love—"America the Beautiful."

Think About It

1. Why was Pikes Peak important to so many people?

2. How did Pike feel about the mountain when he first saw it?

3. The beauty of the mountain inspired Katharine Lee Bates to write a song. Think of a beautiful place you have been to or have seen in pictures. Write a poem about that place.

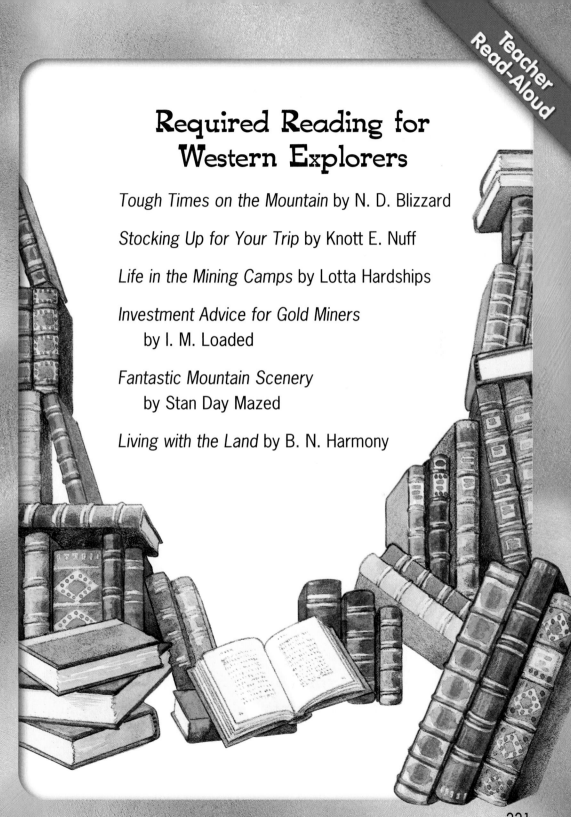

Required Reading for Western Explorers

Tough Times on the Mountain by N. D. Blizzard

Stocking Up for Your Trip by Knott E. Nuff

Life in the Mining Camps by Lotta Hardships

Investment Advice for Gold Miners
by I. M. Loaded

Fantastic Mountain Scenery
by Stan Day Mazed

Living with the Land by B. N. Harmony

AN AMERICAN LEGEND

by Sharon Fear   illustrated by Gerald McDermott

One day Pecos Bill looked out over Texas and decided it was time to move on.

True, Texas had given him plenty from the time he was a little bitty baby. Hadn't the coyotes of Texas taken him in and raised him when he got bumped off his parents' wagon?

But Bill had repaid Texas. Hadn't he created the cowboy life, holding the first roundup and inventing the lariat and other gadgets?

Hadn't he tamed all the Texas tornadoes by riding them into the ground? Why, a stampeding herd of thirsty giant mosquitoes was about the only trouble left in Texas!

That was the problem. Texas was just too tame for the untamed spirit of Pecos Bill.

"I reckon we'll head west," Bill said to his horse, "and set up a brand-new ranch."

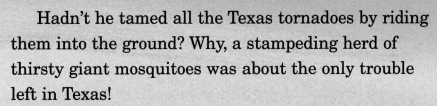

Bill went and claimed some land called New Mexico that he figured would do for his new ranch. Then he said to his horse, "I reckon we'll need cowhands."

Bill asked around. "I need men who are rough, tough, untamed, impolite, and disagreeable! In other words, real cowboys!"

"There's a wild bunch fitting all your requirements right up that canyon," said an old-timer.

"Much obliged!" said Bill. He tipped his ten-gallon hat and off he rode.

On the way up the canyon, Bill's horse got spooked. It bucked off Bill and his saddle and headed for home. Right in Bill's path was a rattlesnake of impossible size!

Old softhearted Bill let the snake have the first bite. Then he hollered, "Enough of this nonsense! I'm Pecos Bill, and you're a snake sandwich!"

Bill jumped on the rattler, tied it in knots, and flung it around his neck. "I was needing a new whip to crack," he said, very pleased.

Just then a wildcat of impossible size sprang upon Bill and tried to chew his head off.

Bill was rather annoyed. He jumped up, bellowing, "I'm Pecos Bill, and you're a wildcat sandwich!"

This might have meant tragedy for the cat, but with his horse gone, Bill needed something to ride. Before that wildcat knew what was happening, Bill threw his saddle on it and jumped aboard. He rode that cat, bucking and screeching, till it was meek as a kitten.

"Thanks," said Bill. "I enjoyed that."

Bill rode on until he saw some men boiling up beans and coffee over a campfire. They were as big as grizzlies and twice as mean-looking. That may have been because they were surrounded by swirling clouds of mosquitoes. Bill cracked his rattlesnake whip, and the pesky critters hightailed it out of there.

"Howdy, boys," said Bill. "I'm mighty hungry and thirsty. How about a ration of that grub?"

He reached into the boiling beans, grabbed some, and gobbled them. He tipped up the coffeepot and swigged down the boiling brew.

"Now, boys," he said, wiping his chin with a prickly pear cactus, "who's boss around here?"

They looked at the man who rode a wildcat, cracked a rattlesnake whip, swallowed boiling grub, and used a cactus for a napkin. Those cowpokes knew that this was a fateful moment for them.

"You are!" they said.

From then on those boys were as loyal as puppies to Bill. They helped him set up one ranch and then moved on with him to another. Just as the legends about Pecos Bill endure, so, too, that ranch endures to this day.

It's called Arizona.

Think About It

1. Why do the wild bunch of men agree to work for Pecos Bill?

2. How do you think the rattlesnake feels when it first sees Pecos Bill? How do you think it feels when he says, "I was needing a new whip to crack"?

3. Choose one of the things Pecos Bill does before he leaves Texas. Write your own story about how Pecos Bill does that.

BUG CATCHERS

by Robert Newell

illustrated by Doug Bowles

BROWN BAT

Brown Bat is my name, and bug-catching is my game! Come along and watch me in action. Marshes are my favorite places to hunt. The **boggiest** marshes, where water oozes up through the mud, are the best because they have the most mosquitoes. I'm headed in the direction of a boggy marsh right now. It's a dark, moonless night, but that won't slow me down.

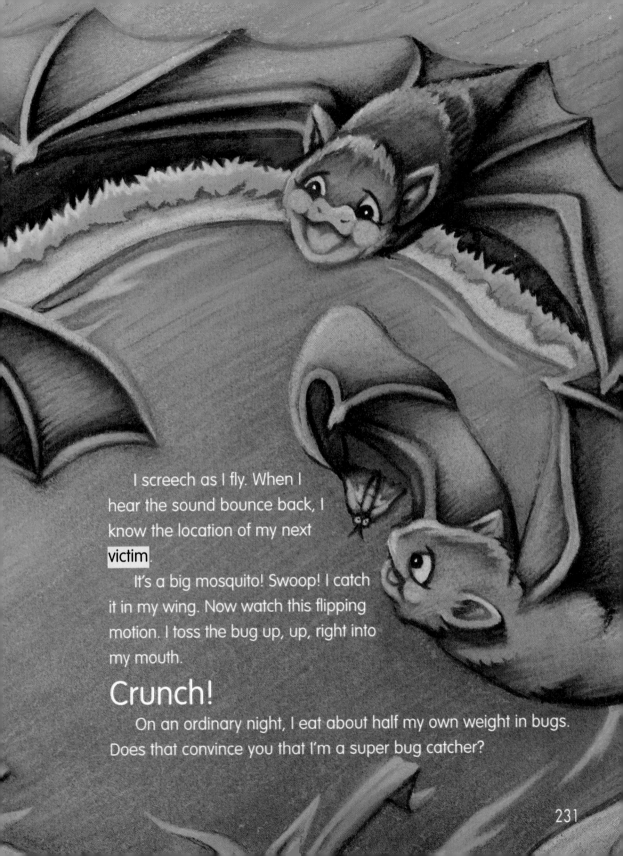

I screech as I fly. When I hear the sound bounce back, I know the location of my next victim.

It's a big mosquito! Swoop! I catch it in my wing. Now watch this flipping motion. I toss the bug up, up, right into my mouth.

Crunch!

On an ordinary night, I eat about half my own weight in bugs. Does that convince you that I'm a super bug catcher?

BOLAS SPIDER

Spiders are bug catchers, too. Ordinary spiders use webs, but not me. I use a different invention.

First I perch on a branch by the garden shed, where fertilizers and bug chemicals are stored. Then I let a silky string ooze from my spinnerets. I add a sticky blob to one end to make a bolas, like the ones South American cowboys use. Then I get into position.

What I do next takes great skill and concentration. I don't see well, but I can feel when moths fly by. They have no notion that I'm here. When one comes close, I quickly toss my bolas in its direction.

I got one!

The moth is tangled in the bolas string. When I pull it in, it's dinner time!

Sometimes I wrap my catch in silk and hang it up to eat later. These roll-ups make great convenience foods for days when I accidentally miss with my bolas. I simply inject a little of my bug-dissolving solution into a prepackaged meal. Then I sip up a delicious dinner.

PRAYING MANTIS

Why fly back and forth all night or struggle with a tangled, sticky string? I catch bugs by holding still and letting them come to me.

First I have to make a decision about where to wait. Today I station myself on a twig near the ground.

I sit motionless, still as a stone. I have five eyes, and my good vision helps me watch for victims.

Here comes a beetle!

I wait, and I wait some more. When the beetle is very close, I pounce. Each of my front legs snaps shut at the joint like a steel trap. The beetle's reaction is to kick and wiggle, but it's useless for it to struggle. I will never let go of my dinner.

I will eat the beetle, but I will still be hungry. I am always hungry. Luckily, there are always more bugs.

OTHER BUG CATCHERS

I catch bugs, too, but I have no intention of eating any. No chocolate-covered ants for me, thank you! I just look at the bugs and let them go.

Anteaters slurp up ants. Fish and frogs gulp down flies. Foxes avoid starvation by eating grubs when they must. All these carnivorous creatures help keep the insect population down, and I'm convinced that's a good thing. After all, how many mosquitoes and flies do you want in your backyard?

Thank you, bug catchers!

Think About It

1. How do a brown bat, a bolas spider, and a praying mantis catch bugs?

2. How does the girl who catches bugs feel about the animal bug catchers? How can you tell?

3. Imagine that you're a mosquito. Write about how you feel when you see a brown bat heading toward you. What do you do? What finally happens?

Air Force Kids

by Sal Ortega   illustrated by Tom Foty

Dear Paul,

Our teacher interrupted classes today to share your letter with us. She liked your idea of writing to investigate what your new environment will be like. I volunteered to write back to you. Air Force kids need to stick together!

In three months, we'll welcome you to our class. Until then, you can ask me about Spain and our base. It's a nice place— you'll like it here.

What's it like in Alaska? Not one kid in Grade 4 has been stationed in Alaska. We're all curious about it.

Your future classmate,

Ricardo Ramos

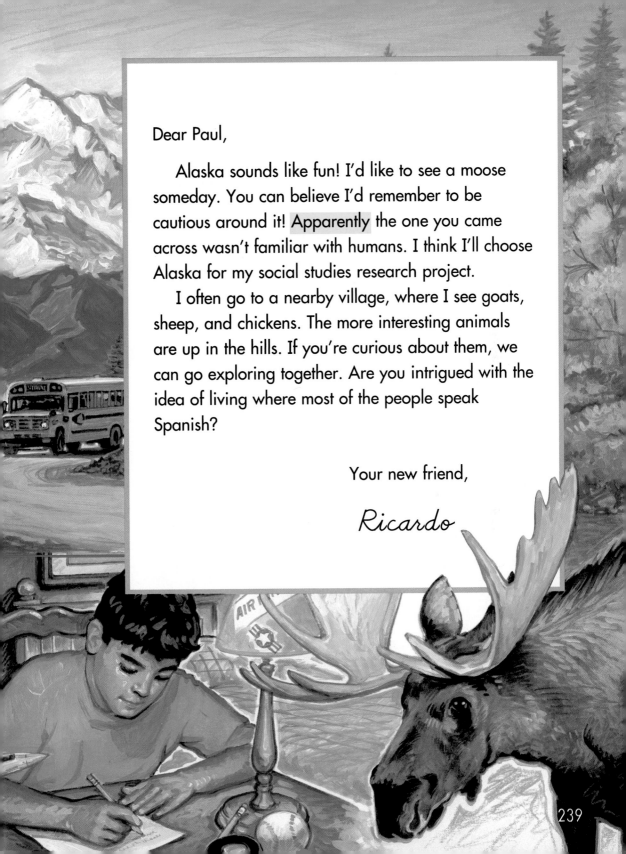

Dear Paul,

Alaska sounds like fun! I'd like to see a moose someday. You can believe I'd remember to be cautious around it! Apparently the one you came across wasn't familiar with humans. I think I'll choose Alaska for my social studies research project.

I often go to a nearby village, where I see goats, sheep, and chickens. The more interesting animals are up in the hills. If you're curious about them, we can go exploring together. Are you intrigued with the idea of living where most of the people speak Spanish?

Your new friend,

Ricardo

239

Dear Paul,

I'll gladly help you with Spanish. I'm surprised that you've never been out of the States. I've never been <u>in</u> them! I was born on a base in Germany. When I was four, we shipped out to Turkey, and then we were transferred here when I was seven. That makes me an American who hasn't been in America! I suppose we'll be sent there someday.

Thanks for the photos of your school. The decor of your classroom and corridor seems very similar to ours. Maybe all the Air Force schools are the same.

Your Air Force buddy,

Ricardo

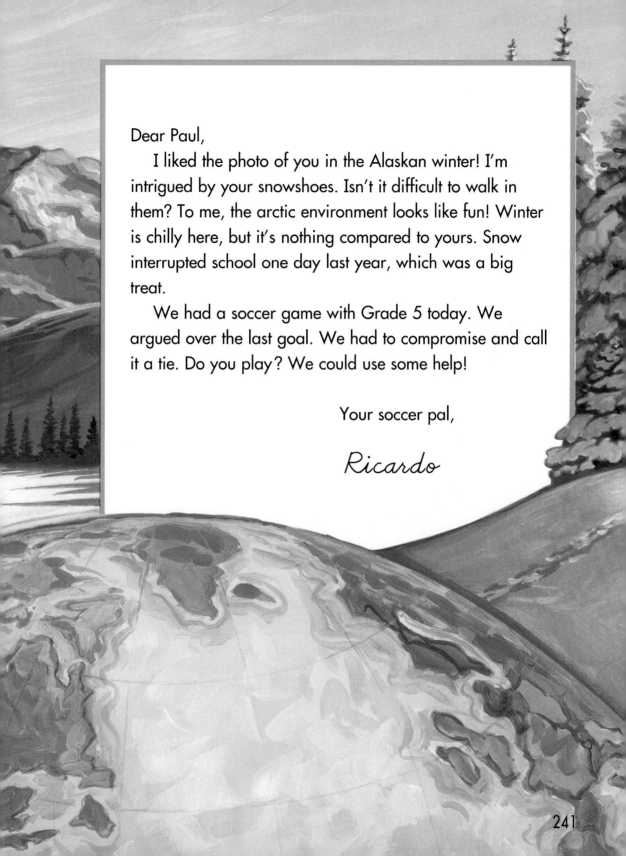

Dear Paul,

I liked the photo of you in the Alaskan winter! I'm intrigued by your snowshoes. Isn't it difficult to walk in them? To me, the arctic environment looks like fun! Winter is chilly here, but it's nothing compared to yours. Snow interrupted school one day last year, which was a big treat.

We had a soccer game with Grade 5 today. We argued over the last goal. We had to compromise and call it a tie. Do you play? We could use some help!

Your soccer pal,

Ricardo

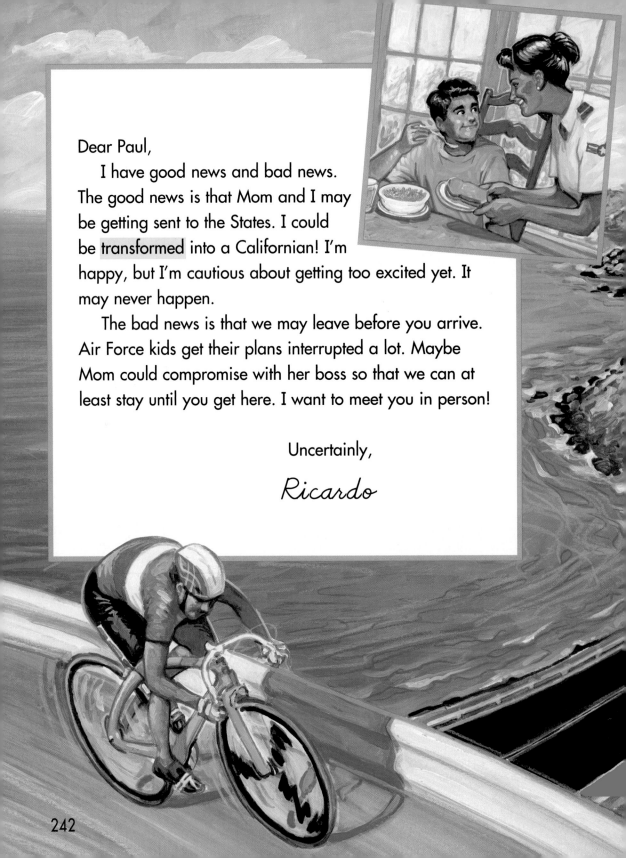

Dear Paul,

I have good news and bad news. The good news is that Mom and I may be getting sent to the States. I could be transformed into a Californian! I'm happy, but I'm cautious about getting too excited yet. It may never happen.

The bad news is that we may leave before you arrive. Air Force kids get their plans interrupted a lot. Maybe Mom could compromise with her boss so that we can at least stay until you get here. I want to meet you in person!

Uncertainly,

Ricardo

Dear Paul,

Something fantastic has happened! Our move to California has been postponed for a year. I'm so happy because now I'll get to meet you in person. We'll have an entire year to do things together.

So you're a Californian yourself! Which base were you born on there? This is great—you can tell me all about California before I move there.

Being an Air Force kid has its advantages. You're coming to Spain at a terrific time. Our World Cup soccer team will be playing at our stadium. We can go together, and you'll see why soccer is so popular!

Enthusiastically,

Ricardo

Dear Paul,

Yes, you'll need to teach me more about baseball. I know it's very popular in California.

I'm excited that you're coming next week! The kids in my class are, too. We feel as if we know you from your letters. You'll finally see my Alaska research project.

You have a long journey ahead of you, but Air Force kids are used to that!

Call me when you get to the base, and I'll give you a tour of the neighborhood.

See you soon,

Ricardo

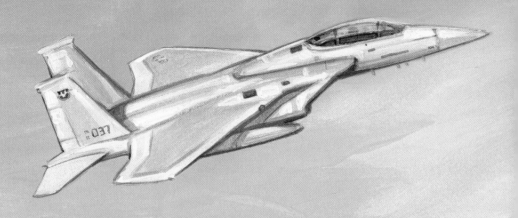

Think About It

1. Why does Ricardo want to stay in Spain until Paul arrives?

2. How do you think Paul will feel on his first day of school in Spain? Why?

3. After Ricardo moves to California, Paul writes him a letter from Spain. Write the letter Paul sends.